Praise for the KGB Bar poetry series
The KGB Bar Book

"KGB has, in its curators and comperes, th[
knock down the walls of the anthology war[
from poet, unleashing a vitality that floods this volume like a good
rendering."

— BOB HOLMAN

"The feel of the room brought back my poet youth in the seventies—that
same rush hour ambiance and who's who excitement and an equiva-
lently imaginative combining of poets."

— HONOR MOORE

"Despite all the smoke and noise from outside, the presence in such prox-
imity of so many poets I admire made it feel as though the audience
were a giant, ideal ('star-infested') ear, hearing everything I wanted them
to hear and more. It was exhilarating."

— CHARLES NORTH

"Everything about the shabby place holds the vicious honesty of art pas-
sionately made, so poets behave themselves in an uncommon luxury of
self-awareness and even kindness toward an audience so discriminating
that it selects second by second the true from the false step."

— MOLLY PEACOCK

"In spite of the bar's sinister name, it has a dark crimson-walled smoky air
of high security in the best sense: a virtual womb of poetry and good writ-
ing, a safe house of camaraderie and kinship between the writers and the
audience. This is not a place to take for granted."

— BILL WADSWORTH

"The pre–Russian Revolutionary locale gives the gathering a committed,
not to say conspiratorial air, and it somehow manages to foster a true
sense of camaraderie, experimentation, and open exchange between
readers and audience. I've seldom enjoyed an evening of poetry and
friendship more."

— JONATHAN GALASSI

THE KGB BAR

Book of Poems

Also by David Lehman

The Daily Mirror: A Journal in Poetry

The Best American Poetry (annual series): 1988–2000

The Last Avant-Garde

Valentine Place

Signs of the Times

Operation Memory

An Alternative to Speech

The Line Forms Here

The Big Question

Ecstatic Occasions, Expedient Forms

The Perfect Murder

Also by Star Black

Balefire

October for Idas

Waterworn

Double Time

THE KGB BAR

Book of Poems

EDITED BY DAVID LEHMAN
AND STAR BLACK

With photographs by Star Black
and an introduction by David Lehman

Perennial
An Imprint of HarperCollins*Publishers*

FIRST EDITION

Designed by Nicola Ferguson

Library of Congress Cataloging-in-Publication Data has been applied for.

ISBN 0-688-17109-5

00 01 02 03 04 BP 10 9 8 7 6 5 4 3 2 1

Editors' Note

This anthology reflects the first three seasons of the KGB Bar poetry series: spring 1997, fall 1997, and spring 1998. The contributors' notes give the dates of the poets' appearances at KGB. The photographs were taken by Star Black from December 1997 through May 1999. The captions were written by David Lehman.

This is an opportune time to acknowledge with thanks the poets who have read for us too recently to be included in these pages. We present their names here in the order in which they read in our series: Ron Padgett, Rosanne Wasserman, Julia Kasdorf, Charles Bernstein, Carole Maso, Philip Levine, Deborah Garrison, Harry Mathews, Alberto Mobilio, Claudia Rankine, Vincent Katz, Joan Larkin, Jaime Manrique, Robert Hershon, Bill Zavatsky, Bruce Andrews, C. D. Wright, James Tate, Dara Wier, Lucie Brock-Broido, Liam Rector, Forrest Gander, Marjorie Welish, Donald Hall, Bob Perelman, John Godfrey, John Koethe, Ed Barrett, Michael Malinowitz, Gyorgyi Voros, Sharon Olds, Denis Nurkse, Jerome Sala, Nicholas Christopher, Marie Ponsot, Gerald Stern, Tomaz Salamun, Thomas Sayers Ellis, Grace Schulman, Brenda Shaughnessy, C. K. Williams, Douglas Goetsch, Phillis Levin, Jennifer Barber, Mark Bibbins, Maggie Nelson, Daniel Halpern, Prageeta Sharma, James Cummins, Carolyn Kizer, Frank Lima, and Michael Schmidt.

October 1999

Contents

Preamble

Located on the second floor of a tenement at 85 East Fourth Street in the East Village of New York City, the KGB Bar is not an easy place to find. The small neon sign high above the stoop goes unnoticed by most passersby. So if you're looking for the place, you have to look hard. Most people come for the first time only because they have a friend who has brought them.

The bar itself is a single room that retains much of the character it had when it was a speakeasy during Prohibition—and a Lucky Luciano joint. With its original tin ceiling and stained-glass Beaux Arts cabinetry, it has the look and feel of a century ago. Its obscure location has been its secret blessing. With little commercial potential, the integrity of its interior has not been destroyed by commerce, gutted and rebuilt, the way its ground-floor neighbors' have. The interior has changed only superficially.

Now its walls are red. Posters of the Soviet triumph over Nazi fascism dating back to World War II, photographs of Brezhnev and the Supreme Soviet, paintings of Taras Schevchenko and Ivan Franko, flags from St. Petersburg, and sculptures of Tolstoy and Lenin now adorn the interior. A blood red flag with hammer and sickle hangs from the ceiling.

The KGB Bar is a living museum to its own history.

From 1948 until I took over in 1992, the barroom and the building itself belonged to a Ukrainian socialist social club. The posters, the photographs, the paintings, the flags—they were all there but tucked away somewhere and out of view. What better way to bring an intellectually curious public to an obscure location than to give that public something authentic? So the posters and photographs were framed (by maximum-security mental patients, a matter of economics and a much longer story) and hung alongside the paintings and flags, and the sculptures were placed on countertops—to allow the room's history to continue its march through time.

But do not doubt that the KGB Bar is a capitalist enterprise; it is a bar.

Still, in deference to its socialist past, KGB offers readings by some of America's finest living poets and writers—*free* to the masses—although drinks are sold and drinking is encouraged.

Hey, a man's got to make a buck.

Long ago, before I was of drinking age, I was a romantic. I thought of bars as places where people went to share ideas, art, and culture—the hangouts of the Beat generation. When finally I became a young man-about-town, the bars were about pinkie rings or televised sports. There was no place like the KGB Bar.

And there still isn't.

I want to thank David Lehman and Star Black for their very capable leadership of the Monday night poetry series. They have made it a success in every sense of the word. I also want to thank my friends and investors, Richard Cogan and his brother Bruce, whom I have known since childhood, Ed Sukman, Carla Sarr, Jerry Weinberger, and of course Melvin Jules Bukiet, like myself a writer, who conceived with me the idea for original reading programs at the KGB Bar. I also want to thank Ken Foster for his excellent work on the mostly fiction *KGB Bar Reader*, which was released in 1998.

Denis Woychuk

Introduction

BY DAVID LEHMAN

Among the hippest, perhaps the hottest, and surely the most unlikely venue for poetry in New York City these days is a dimly lit second-floor bar festooned with defunct Soviet icons in the East Village. So say lots of people. In its 1999 "Best of New York" issue, New York magazine named KGB a "faux-underground Commie theme bar–cum–writers' clubhouse," "the top choice among literati of all ages" in the category of "Places to Be Read To." The New York Times has run more than one article to the same effect. "What began as a grungy salon of the downtown lit pack has begun to develop an out-size reputation," the paper recently reported in an article on KGB headlined "A Cold War Relic Is a Literary Hot Spot."

Star Black and I, codirectors of Monday Night Poetry at KGB, are sometimes asked to account for the popularity of the series. In response we cite the poets who have read for us. The discussion doesn't end there—the bar and its atmosphere and the quality of our audience must have plenty to do with it—but it begins with the poets. The KGB Bar Book of Poems will give you an idea of who these poets are and what makes them so worthy of a hearing. Each poet who read at KGB during our first three seasons has contributed a poem to this volume—in most cases a poem that was tested out on a KGB audience. The contributors were invited to supplement their poems and biographical notes with anecdotes about the best or worst thing ever to happen to them at a reading or with reflections on readings in general. Half the poets have obliged us, and one, J. D. McClatchy, has written a poem on the theme for this occasion. In addition we include an abundant sampling of Star Black's photographs of poets and patrons at the bar. To readers who could not be there in person, this combination of poems, prose, and pictures may convey something of the excitement of a poetry reading at KGB—and of that moment in particular when the bartender turns off the music, an anticipatory hush settles over the crowd, and the poets of the week pull out their manuscripts.

At KGB the poets feel free to read their latest writings, about which they have the most passionate feelings and are perhaps most undecided. This sense of newness, of doubt and of risk, is one reason for the success of the series. For the audience, it is a special pleasure to be among the first to hear the new work of an admired figure. For the poet, it is an equal or greater pleasure (though sometimes a nerve-racking one) to read to an audience one esteems—an audience in which, on any given evening, you might find some of the contributors to this volume as well as other practicing poets and artists. The spirit of the new is there amid the bar smells, the smoke, the martinis, the old furnishings and older soundtrack (the Jimmy Dorsey Orchestra's rendition of "So Rare," for example), and the red drapes over the windows.

It is an arresting irony that a bar bearing the acronym of the Soviet intelligence agency should celebrate freedom in several senses. No one—neither the organizers nor the poets who read for us—is paid. There is no admission fee, no cover charge, no minimum. The readings are free, and this fact may paradoxically be what impels poets from near or remote places to read without recompense in our series. We can and do capitalize, of course, on New York City's magnetism and its centrality. We know that Richard Howard lives a few blocks away, that a short cab ride separates us from John Ashbery, and that illustrious others, wherever they may reside, have schedules that may bring them to Gotham at some point in the year. Of the contributors to this volume, Frank Bidart flew in from Boston, Nin Andrews from Cleveland, Dana Gioia from San Francisco, and Erin Belieu from St. Louis. Charles Simic drove down from New Hampshire, Carl Dennis from Buffalo. (The tradition continues. In the past several months, James Tate and Dara Wier came from Amherst, Massachusetts, Bob Perelman from Philadelphia, Julia Kasdorf from Camp Hill, Pennsylvania, and Thomas Sayers Ellis from Cleveland.) In the brief interval between winning the National Book Critics Circle Award and the Pulitzer Prize in 1998, Charles Wright flew in from Virginia to read on the same bill as his close friend Mark Strand, visiting from Chicago.

The heterogeneity of our list speaks for itself. We can have, in the same season, poets of the New York School and the Beat revival, Language poets and New Formalists, experimentalists of various stripes, exemplars of styles and movements not thought to be compatible. We are ecumenical, inconsistent, deliberately nonprogrammatic. We want poems that are, in Duke Ellington's phrase, "beyond category." We believe that the spirit of the new provides enough of a unifying principle and that sooner or later all factions may be represented — and transcended.

When the KGB Bar served as headquarters for the Kraine Society, a Ukrainian social club used as a clandestine meeting place for Cold War Communists and socialists, the walls were painted red. Red they remain. Flickering candles illuminate the portraits of Lenin and Brezhnev, hammer-and-sickle flags, stark photographs of Soviet factories, sketches of the Russian countryside, and World War II Communist anti-Nazi posters. All this is evidence, perhaps, of postmodernism in action: What had been a meaningful symbol turns into style or decor, emptied of meaning, and the past survives in a parodic form, as though to illustrate the thesis that history repeats itself as farce. Or perhaps it is "retro

Commie chic" in the service of "night owl capitalism," as the *New York Times*'s Glenn Collins suggests. There is a tradition of naming places after great battles. The Austerlitz train station in Paris is named for one of Napoleon's victories, the Waterloo station in London for one of Napoleon's defeats. Flaunting the initials of an institution that persecuted poets, the KGB Bar would seem a special case, a way of turning a symbol of terror into a site for creative freedom. We drink to freedom (and, some would say, to the Dionysian triumph of the Manhattan cocktail over the Molotov kind). Be that as it may, audience and reader are invariably amused when a poem referring to the actual, infamous KGB is read aloud at the KGB Bar. Such a moment occurred when L. S. Asekoff read "Casa Blanca" (in which a paranoid narrator relates that "it is rumored/the KGB/plans to clear me/for radiation work/all over Russia") and again when Bruce Andrews made mention of "the KGB honeymoon guide" in his "Millennial Project." During the first season of Monday Night Poetry at KGB, people were offered a free drink if they could explain why several trendy nightspots in the city bore the names of failed Soviet institutions. The best answer we heard was, "Because we won the Cold War."

At a KGB reading the poet stands behind an old wooden podium. No microphone is used; there is nothing artificial about the KGB experience—though occasionally a camera crew from an all-news TV station turns up to give things a little jolt. The noises of the city (fire engines, honking horns, car alarms, the occasional shout in the street) punctuate the poetry, or compete with it, and seem indispensable to the aesthetic experience, as in a John Cage composition. Or maybe the theater company on the floor below is rehearsing a fight or dance scene. Curiously, even things that limit your ability to hear—which you might have thought decisive at a poetry reading—seem not to diminish the audience's pleasure. How else to understand the willingness of people, on our most crowded evenings, to stand on the landing outside the red room or even down the rickety staircase, avidly listening though hearing, one supposes, mere fragments?

People seem to be addicted to poetry readings. More and more since, in their differing ways, Dylan Thomas and Allen Ginsberg electrified audiences in the 1950s, the poetry reading has supplanted the page as the site for the encounter of poem and reader. Some would lament this tendency. One problematic effect, Elizabeth Bishop pointed out, is "the fear of boring," or the related temptation to pander to the audience. T. S. Eliot confided that when he gave a poetry reading he felt as if guilty of "indecent exposure." James Dickey felt that giving poetry readings in America "sure killed off poor Dylan Thomas," who "didn't write even *one* poem in the last six years of his life. Everybody *loved* him; he was screwing all the coeds in America, drinking all the whiskey, and he'd get up and read his poems, and then he'd go on and read them somewhere else. He got a lot of dough for it. I mean, what incentive for him to write *was* there? To survive, a poet has to find some way of maintaining his original enthusiasm for *poetry*, not for the by-products of poetry, not for the fringe benefits of poetry, but for *it.*" In a posthumous poem displaying his mordant wit, William Matthews exclaims, "I hate/poetry readings and the dreaded verb/'to share.' Let me share this knife with your throat,/suggested Mack."

At the same time, it must be acknowledged that the poetry reading boom of the nineties—perhaps especially the downtown variety situated in bars and cafés rather than on college campuses—signals the engagement of a new generation of young people, who associate poetry with its oral presentation. To public readings and their offshoots—competitive slams, hip-hop poems, and such—goes much of the credit for the expansion of poetry's audience. As for the charge that poetry readings are impure, one need only turn to an enthusiastic account of a reading that proved decisive in a young poet's life. Ted Berrigan's journals record his responses to hearing Allen Ginsberg's "Kaddish" ("It was a very good poem, and a brilliant reading"), Kenneth Koch ("Koch reminds me of Nijinsky as Groucho Marx"), and Frank O'Hara ("His wit is sharp, brittle, sneering often, yet he is tender, gentle, loving") in New York City in 1961 and 1962. Dara Wier, after she read at KGB in February 1999, told me about "having seen otherwise disinterested listeners become entranced" at a reading. "Which reminds me," she continued, "of the first poetry reading I attended: W. S. Merwin reading in 1968 from *The Lice* in Baton Rouge, Louisiana. Can you imagine? In a darkened auditorium with good stage lighting, too much. I stopped off at a pizza joint on my way to that reading and had my little booth all to myself and a collection of short stories—I think K. A. Porter's *Flowering Judas*—and lo and behold I sensed behind my back the poet's host and the poet himself. All I knew of him then was one poem, 'Lemuel's Blessing'; needless to say I shivered. Not even speaking to this otherworldly presence caused me, as they say, paroxysmal embarrassment. And the rest of the evening, well, that was the anniversary of my death. (I was well past disinterested, but the depth of my amazement that living poets walked the earth not to mention ate food in neighborhoods gave me the onset of aphasia. Lucky me. And lucky I'm sure thousands more before and since.)"

The poetry reading is such a pervasive phenomenon today that a culture and a literature have sprung up around it. People who attend readings are familiar, for example, with what Julia Kasdorf calls "the three-poem warning"—the moment when the poet announces, "Just three more poems," as if to reassure a clock-conscious audience. Many poets know well the futile gesture of checking their watches to see how long they have read—futile, because they failed to check their watches when they began. Nearly everyone seems to have a favorite horror story or amusing anecdote. The humiliation of the poet is a recurring theme. "When I read my poems at a small college in Minnesota, the dean led me to the auditorium telling me that he had forgotten something," Donald Hall told me at a lunch following his evening at KGB. "I was to read for half my usual time, because at this assembly the college was choosing its homecoming queen. I adjusted without difficulty. The auditorium was crowded with students, and at a later lunch several faculty told me that they had entered the hall surprised to see so many people come out for poetry. When I finished reading to a tolerant if indifferent audience, last year's homecoming queen ascended the platform, ready to introduce this year's candidates. She began, And now comes the moment you've all been waiting for . . .' "

Unusual introductions form a subgenre of their own. In the early 1970s Elizabeth Bishop gave a reading at Brown University at which (she wrote in a letter to James Merrill) her introducer said "he'd spent the whole day with a graduate student who'd gone mad, trying to get him to go to a hospital, I think. To calm him, he had read him my poetry." After implying that Bishop's poetry had the attributes of a tranquilizer, the introducer went on to observe that "the young madman had become convinced that he—the madman—had written my poems," Bishop recalled. "Then 'Ladies & Gentlemen, Miss B.' "

Poems about poetry readings have proliferated in recent years. I have a special fondness for "At the Poetry Reading" by John Brehm, a regular at our Monday night series. The poem begins:

I can't keep my eyes off the poet's
wife's legs,—they're so much more
beautiful than anything he might

be saying, though I'm no longer
in a position really to judge,
having stopped listening some time ago.

Rather than listen to workshop-produced poems about childhood, "the loss of innocence," and science, Brehm's persona gives his attention to the "wife's fluid,/rhythmic, lusciously curved, black-/stockinged legs." The poem concludes:

My God, why doesn't he write poems about her!
He will, no doubt, once she leaves him,
leaves him for another poet, perhaps,
the observant, uninnocent one, who knows
a poem when it sits down in a room with him.

The anecdotes included in this book tell of readings that have become the stuff of legend (James Schuyler at DIA in November 1988) or high gossip (Robert Lowell getting booed off the stage at St. Mark's Church or being introduced as a dead man in Cambridge, England). There are the archetypal nightmares: the one in which a certain somebody in the audience turns the poet's knees to jelly (David Trinidad), the one in which nobody turns up (Thomas Lux), the one in which the poet arrives at the podium without his or her poems (Tom Carey, Lucy Grealy, Charles North), and the one in which the poet's "inexpertly wrapped wraparound skirt" goes "dashing to the ground" (Erin Belieu). Hal Sirowitz was pelted with a beer bottle during a reading. "And when I complained to the organizer he claimed it was a sign of affection." There are special risks for organizers and introducers. Bill Wadsworth needed the help of the New York Police Department's A-Team when the Ayatollah Khomeini ordered the assassination of the author scheduled to read in Bill's series that week. Susan Wheeler, who taught poetry in a maximum-security prison in Vermont, recalls driving three intimidating prisoners to their first radio performance. Their terror at the prospect dwarfed her own as their designated and unarmed driver.

The popularity of readings has changed the art itself in subtle and overt ways. One effect of poetry readings as a literary and cultural phenomenon is that they make the invisible reader visible. Our vocabulary registers the change. On the printed page, the poet speaks to the reader; in the public space, the poet has become the reader speaking to the audience. The performative element has been elevated. Poetry becomes a communal event not only in the sense that it can serve a social, political, or religious function (Allen Ginsberg chanting William Blake's "Songs of Innocence" at the Washington Monument in 1970) but equally in the sense that a symphony or concerto is an event: it takes place in time, in front of an audience, and it becomes arguable at least that its value and meaning are inextricably bound up with its mode of presentation.

Why do we go to poetry readings? Before evoking some of the most memorable evenings in his fifteen seasons as director of the poetry program at the Ninety-second Street Y, Karl Kirchwey states the literary rationale. Readings establish a "primal connection" between poet and audience, Kirchwey argues. Poetry has the power to explain itself "when read well aloud." Bob Holman, maestro of slams at the Nuyorican Poets Cafe, goes further. "A poem doesn't happen till it's heard," Holman writes. The nonliterary case for readings is presented wittily by Douglas Crase: "Why get out of bed and go to a reading? Sometimes there is a party afterward. This I discovered at the first reading I attended on my own, in a small college town, from the helpful professor who said there is a party afterward but I can't take you because you are uninvited. It is a joy to come to New York and go where you are uninvited." As curators of the KGB poetry series, where the unin-

vited are always welcome, Star Black and I are immensely grati-
ied that so many contributors to this volume have tossed bouquets
our way.

Many readers (and listeners) are smitten with the romance of
the city's bohemian past. We know that New York's rich cultural
history is bound up with such downtown bars and dives as the
Cedar Tavern (where the Abstract Expressionists held court), the
San Remo (where the young poets of the New York School hung
out in the 1950s), and the Five Spot (where Frank O'Hara heard
Billie Holiday "whisper a song along the keyboard" and captured
the moment in a marvelous elegy). Recalling the first poetry read-
ing he ever attended—at Forlini's, an upper Broadway bar near
Columbia—Bob Holman jokes that "a next-to-unusable space" is
"a poetry kind of place." But Holman reminds us, too, that the
Village Vanguard, world-famous as a shrine of jazz, began as a
poetry bar. Poetry belongs in bars—it has as much right to be
there as in universities. Monday nights at the KGB Bar remind
Honor Moore of a bar called Dr. Generosity's, where poetry pros-
pered in the 1970s, while Jonathan Galassi invokes "the fabulous
heroic underground New York of O'Hara and Schuyler and
Denby, of Ginsberg, Corso, and LeRoi Jones," in the 1950s and
early 1960s. How wonderful to speculate that people years hence
may look back at KGB in the same fond light or half-light. As
Galassi declared during his KGB reading, "I feel I'm a part of
history."

THE KGB BAR

Book of Poems

Nin Andrews

Nin Andrews is the author of *The Book of Orgasms* and *Spontaneous Breasts*. She lives in Poland, Ohio, with her husband and two children. She wrote "Poets on Poets" during the Associated Writing Programs' annual conference in Washington, D.C., in 1997. She read at KGB on December 8, 1997.

A radiant Nin Andrews flew in from Cleveland to read from her underground classic The Book of Orgasms.

1

POETS ON POETS

—I'm pretending not to see him so I can eat my lunch.

—But who reads that shit? About as true to life as a velvet grape.

—I think he judges poetry with his dick. And poets, too.

—What's the scoop on her? Is that her husband, or is he just hanging out in her hotel room for the duration?

—Personally I prefer not to think about his dick.

—His latest work, especially the poems about his dead father, begins to sound human.

—Think of it as a conductor's baton.

—Granted, she wins *all* the prizes, but talk about grandiose.

—The latest inductee into the goddess cult. Like back in the sixties when sex and war were the metaphors for consciousness-raising.

—I bet they're really confessional, and she's a total pervert too.

—He knows how to network, who to climb, and when. Timing is everything.

—Insomnia, maybe chronic fatigue syndrome. I think it's just frayed nerves.

—I always admired your work but can't figure why it's been so marginalized.

—You want my phone number?

—The illusion of the narrative appears in your work, but there's really a thread of the unspoken narrative, right?

—Are you married? Do you have children?

—Never even answered my inquiries, the pompous bastard.

—That's really sweet. Thank you.

—I think I have a blind spot when it comes to his work.

—Must be great to get away.

—I don't know why they don't just fire the asshole.

—Reminds me of a gilt frame with no picture inside.

—She's eloquent enough, a nice cocktail poet.

—Did you see what he was wearing?

—She says it's none of my business what she writes.

—Poetry is a private affair. A kind of masturbation. An endless self-portrait.

—So what if he is another excellent specimen of the dead father poets.

—Where are the dead mother poets?

—I like the way you think.

—Yet another vapid, beautiful wind-blown babe-poet for the cover of AWP.

—Let's go out for a beer somewhere.

—I sure wouldn't want to live in his skin.

—A local dive would be nice.

—The way I see it, you're better off not getting famous too soon.

—I never even send out my work.

Sarah Arvio

Sarah Arvio, a poet and translator, lives sometimes in New York, sometimes in Paris, and works as a conference translator for the United Nations. "Mirrors (No. XIX)" belongs to a sequence of poems entitled "Visits from the Seventh," numbers I through XI of which appeared in *The Paris Review*, won the 1997 Bernard F. Conners Prize for the long poem, and were reprinted in *The Best American Poetry 1998*. She has won a National Endowment for the Arts translator's fellowship. Three stories she translated were included in *The Oxford Book of Latin American Short Stories* (1997). She read at KGB on February 23, 1998.

MIRRORS

(NO. XIX)

A while later that night they flurried in;
some were humming and laughing nervously.
"Have you assessed the deep indecency

most of you tend to feel at having sex
before the spread of a mirror? As though
another couple were in the room and

couldn't help now and then peering over
at your pleasure and peeking in your eyes?"
"Who wouldn't flush red at the sight of those

other two bodies moving in rhythm
both with each other and also with you?"
"But under that blush lies a deeper one —

the subliminal, sublunary sense
of being observed from another sphere."
"Thus the preference for modest mirrors

hung well above the scene and frame of love,
expanding the sense of the room's depth, yes,
but offering at best an oblique view

to a watcher at a higher vantage."
"And note that those who get an extra thrill
from curling and rolling before mirrors

are voyeurs, or are wanting to be seen
by voyeurs, which amounts to the same thing:
an illicit view of others' pleasure

or illicit exposure of one's own" . . .
And now the riffs of laughter lulled and ceased:
"Despite what pleasure we may derive from

reacquaintance with breasts and balls and lips,
it *is* considered in cosmic bad taste
to show too much sex to the other side."

Is it—I was moved to ask—painfully
nostalgic or tender or even raw
to look in later from a place apart?

Giving a low sigh, one spun and then spoke:
"The convocation of qualms and kisses,
the regrets—the assembly of regrets

for those not loved, for those not loved enough,
and for those who should never have been touched—
what else in this death could be more poignant?

Nothing being left of what might have been
but a half-glance through a glaze of silver . . ."
And here he stopped. No, he could not go on.

Sarah Arvio briefs Verse *coeditor Andrew Zawacki (left) and* lit *poetry editor Mark Bibbins on her recent adventures in Paris and Geneva.*

Years ago, the owner of a restaurant I worked in told me a story about having sex in the mirror-paneled bedroom of a brothel in some foreign country. I felt obliged to listen, for he was, after all, the boss; even though I had been brought up during the liberation wave, and was expected to embrace all forms of experimentation, it seemed smutty, and what, after all, was I supposed to respond? I've always felt that being able to see one's own act of sex was terribly erotic but also a kind of immodesty and sacrilege. After I read this poem and some others in New York last year, a woman in the audience wrung my hands, stared probingly into my eyes, and said, "You gave us your soul." I felt embarrassed and said, "I hope not." I enjoy the notion of mirrors as windows, and of course we speak of eyes as both windows and mirrors of the soul. As a small child, I sometimes hid myself from the bathroom mirror as I climbed out of the bathtub so that I wouldn't be seen. I've also had unnerving dreams in which I'm standing alone before a mirror in which someone unknown stands beside me, looking at me as I look at myself.

SARAH ARVIO

L. S. Asekoff

L. S. Asekoff was born in Boston in 1939 and was raised on the grounds of a state mental hospital where his father was psychiatric director. He coordinates the M.F.A. poetry program at Brooklyn College, where he has taught since the 1960s. He was twice awarded the *American Poetry Review*'s Jerome J. Shestack Prize. His first two books, *Dreams of a Work* (1994) and *North Star* (1997) were published by Orchises Press. He read at KGB on May 5, 1997.

L. S. Asekoff—Lou to friends—pleased the KGB crowd with "Rounding the Horn," which James Tate selected for The Best American Poetry 1997.

WILL

This morning the hibiscus is in bloom, so I stayed in bed late
thinking of ways to repair the wall & kill my mother—muscle relaxants
vets use to put dogs away painlessly or perhaps a pillow,
but that's too Shakespearean, anything to deliver her from
the daily supermarket of misery—children reeking of sex abuse,
old men & women risen from piss-stained rubber sheets & diapers
gliding ever so slowly up & down the aisles, snails
in trails of their own urine. Visiting her at the home
where she's hardly moved or spoken for months,
I could feel her consciousness, not closer but shallower,
as though she were evaporating underneath, slipping away, shallowing
out.
"Mother," I cried, "I miss you." "I miss me, too." She smiled.

When I was a child we summered on the shore. That's me
in my sailor suit with a Raggedy Andy doll. Mother
stayed inside, painting, painting. What? Who knows? Shadows on walls.
She was the world's first abstract depressionist. Oh,
one got used to her self-demeaning manner which was really
criticism in disguise, her malignant negativities
unspoken & sudden disappearances. That was taken when
the whole family rode a glass-topped railway carriage
all the way across the Rockies. We stayed with a cousin in Seattle
who showed us a slum. You are as old as I was then &
I am as old as my father was when he divorced my mother.
What does that prove? Nothing, probably, except the mind's
tireless need for symmetries.

I was eight when Father bought me
my first Kodak. I took careful note of each exposure. Now
it's automatic, the f-stop, the aperture depending only
upon depth of field. Still, I try to keep the light,
positive approach, humorous & inhumane, knowing all the while
my insights are brilliant lies, all lies—the fearless quest
for the fatuous—as though we were all aesthetic objects
to be handled with tongs. This photograph's the embodiment
of my mother's will—flowers raging in the garden,
her shadow & that man standing among Fiesta ware & anger
which puts nails in the eyes, my father. While I no longer believe a
　　father
is someone who brings fire down from the skies, I never fail to cry
over the passage where Coleridge holds his son, Hartley, up to the moon
so he'll always associate it with happiness. Yes, he's my rod
& she's my staff & neither of them comforts me.

This X-ray shows
the dual shadows forming—a cloud, a kidney, a stone—
you can fill in the signifiers & even though we sometimes confuse
occasion with cause, all comes home to roost in the bed
of the cursed progenitor—first fire, then the flood.
Before the First World War, her mother, my grandmother,
worked in the Dixon pencil factory & when the local gigolo
deserted her she prayed to Joseph & the B.V.M. to send her a husband
& they did—a carpenter from the basement storeroom,
& Mother arrived soon after. Still, in photographs, as in life,
the more you figure out the more you are puzzled by
the space between—discontinuities—& dream some completion,

sacrificing everything for the perfect moment: Cartier-
Bresson's Zen snapshots of eternity or Weston riding the cusp
of the last frozen wave—that perpetual scream
that is the siren to our silence.

                              Anyway, there I stood, knee-deep
in begonias, a brick in each hand, unable to think,
trapped inside the bottomless bad infinity
of a woman's unhappiness, when my neighbor's golden retriever
fishes from the pond the gray cat—so innocent of everything.
Animal griefs are cumulative—each little death
adding to the others because in itself somehow so incomplete.
I took this picture, then buried it & went inside to weep
for it, for us, for God . . .

                    My last visit,
I waved the Living Will before him. "Doctor, I am now
my own mother. Her death is my death." He didn't blink.
I guess they get used to it. But it's clear she's crossed some line—
like a dark horse gradually becoming visible.
It leaves me feeling that after-the-funeral energy
before the funeral's even occurred—the desire to dust light
fixtures, scrub floors, rebuild this wall. Last night, I dreamed
her severed hands, her breasts. Look, you can see
how incredibly beautiful she's become, if motionless, mute.
Her eyes flickering slightly in the flash & mouth moving only
when I raise the glass of root beer to her lips.
Her skin has taken on the waxy pallor of saints in decay
as slowly she shows me all the colors of her dying.

Each visit, while she dozes, I pass time with the woman in the
    wheelchair
who smokes platonic cigarettes & is always late,
or else listen to the Alice-in-Wonderland logic
of the man who once wrote the seminal book on that brilliant
Victorian loony who photographed little girls on water—
tactfully avoiding all the while the lingering scent
of sweet Mrs. Benvolio, the shit machine. Sometimes I wonder
what's in her mind. I know we're all a stone's throw away
from satori—that the only illumination is
there's no illumination. The mystery's not what will be
but what has been. Tomorrow, I'll bring her *Good Housekeeping*
just for the Dada of it & this picture of her as a baby,
held in her mother's arms, while her father, my namesake, stands in
    black
                    behind her.

John Brehm, a Monday night regular, says he has a new poem elaborating the view of longtime New Yorker poetry editor Howard Moss that dogs are better than poems.

Poets Elizabeth Willis ("What is happiness? Not sun or sky, and never Plato. A breeze to sweet-talk drunkenness, a song inking up the night") and Peter Gizzi, in town from the left coast, came to KGB to hear Bruce Andrews read from his Millennial Project on Pearl Harbor Day 1998.

John Ashbery

John Ashbery was born in Rochester, New York, in 1927. The most recent of his eighteen books of poetry are *Girls on the Run* (1999) and *Wakefulness* (1998), both from Farrar, Straus and Giroux. *April Galleons* and *Houseboat Days* were also reissued by FSG in 1999. He has been a Guggenheim Fellow, a MacArthur Fellow, and a chancellor of the Academy of American Poets. In 1995 he received the Poetry Society of America's Frost Medal. His *Self-Portrait in a Convex Mirror* received the Pulitzer Prize, the National Book Award, and the National Book Critics Circle Award. He read at KGB on March 10, 1997, and has served as a "guest introducer" on several other occasions.

NEW CONSTRUCTIONS

Boy I can remember when February
gave out and it was all "no quarter"—the sect of the
levellers passed over and was as night and fire
and more peace. He returned in an hour.
Perpetually flummoxed doorkeepers trying to kill
the men who did the migration proceedings
on the evening news
were backed up all the way to the Arctic Circle.

The aunts were out in zones
of cozy brilliance I
noticed with teapots to their names
like birthing, and they could do Finland then.

It was a kind of parenting. I notice they
doubled our salaries. It was all over
by 6 p.m.

Many causes later he came
in and hurt himself. I
saw a lot of cherry bombs. Is this the place
where one foregathers?
If so, what are all the urchins doing?
Oh, she warned it's just to the end of the block
where knee-high tulips pucker and all is reassuring
as they'd rather not have you believe. Does
that clear everything up? Well I think so well I
would like to see the proof of the invitation:
a hand print. I'm so sorry these are inexcusable.
I'll dust myself up, or off;
meanwhile in the clearing they are pouring something.
Do you think you could be kind to come in

and matter where the horse esteems mechanized shortcuts?
Say rather he came in and hurt himself,
and now the bagpipers have nothing left to mourn,
the day just wheezes and goes down a funnel
counterclockwise. It was all just a fit
to have made you start bolt upright
on the steppe terns parted from
with little glovelike cries
awaiting the refrigerator that was to have us all
on its digital menu.

Wait, there are extenuating circumstances
and I myself am just a bum;
whatever came in with the weather
and dematerialized in the corners of the room, just so
am I to myself and others around.
But how do you justify

the crank silhouetted against the sky?
That's just it, I don't; it is all leftovers
and why am I crying
when the boats pass
in the narrow ship channel
with corduroy undies for all the years
I took off from Mrs. Bacon's
and the way they came flooding back at me
like complaints in a gyroscope
or an armillary of vexations.
Then she proposed take this needle
and thread it for the two
messages you have missed.

I'll not start another reptile war;
I look to the end of the komodo dragons thundering overhead.
Otherwise I sleep under the eaves; the cabbages
keep me company at evening, and are all
the society anyone wants. And yes,
I keep up the sewing, the round robin
of Lettergate wherever a spare postal employer
taxes us with unlived puns: *There*

do we stop and pitch camp,
and I'll tell you it's not going to get easier,
only harder.
With that they

took off, just a bundle
of stems to make a totem with.
I sit on the site over and over,
let it absorb hard doing,
piecemeal reconciliations, laundry
marks rubbed out in the wash, seasonal
hares and conviviality and the rest,
the rest.

John Ashbery (right) shows David Lehman his new poem "Merrily We Live."
"I took the title from a 1930s screwball comedy starring Constance
Bennett," he explains. Painter Darragh Park is in the background.

Mary Jo Bang

Mary Jo Bang was born in Waynesville, Missouri, in 1946. She was educated at Northwestern University, Northminster University (London), and Columbia University. Her book of poems, *Apology for Want* (University Press of New England/Middlebury College Press), received the Bakeless Prize and the 1998 Great Lakes Colleges Association New Writers Award. Since 1995 she has been the poetry coeditor of *Boston Review*. She holds the Hodder Fellowship at Princeton University for the 1999–2000 academic year. She read at KGB on March 24, 1997.

IT SAYS, I DID SO

A plaid is formed of yellow block and black,
the nattered weave, an avenue at dawn or dusk.
It gets writ: *I did so*

love you. As if a grid of windows treaded night, as
into darkness—too easy, demon—too vague.
Into absorption. The eyes against themselves.

Shrunken sphere where *this* is twin to *there*.
You let me. Dream last night: a woman and a dress
that's not her own. A man beside a lamp. What

is he? As in life, the silent telephone,
its petty catalogue of equally improbables,
a wave of names each resting on the barren beige

of dirt reduced to dust. Such violence.

Look at this, the scalloped edge cannot escape its rote.

On and on like little wisdoms neck to neck.

Forgetting is out. The cloth turns to anything you wish.

Witness the kiss of interlocking stitch.

These are not artificial tears.

Mary Jo Bang (right) looking serene and glad to be back in the city after a five-month sojourn in Montana. Paul Violi (left) and David Shapiro share the moment.

I have few personal feelings regarding poetry readings and no reading experiences of an engaging extreme (although, as superlatives go, KGB is the reddest place I've ever read). The few feelings I do have can be summed by quoting from a letter from Vivian (Mrs. T. S.) Eliot to Mary Hutchinson (dated March 13, 1918):

It was awfully good of you to ask us to this dance. I have really never disliked having to refuse an invitation so much as I did that. It was so tempting to me. Dances are so few, and as you know, they mean a lot to me. I am trying to earn an honest (for a change) penny, by cinema acting, and have attained an unexpected success. I had to refuse the Sitwell's—last night—for the same reason.

or, sd Tom zphillipd in Yhr zhrsy og s Humumrny[1] dsif,

    omple

           omple
           omple

      they repeat
        and they
          retreat,

[1] (Tom Phillips, *The Heart of a Humument*)

Will there be music? Will there be a crowd? Will there be mooncakes, melon—coconut and cashew?

MARY JO BANG

Judith Baumel

Judith Baumel was born in the Bronx the day after Don Larsen's perfect game in the World Series. Since then she has pursued interests in baseball and poetry separately, with digressions in the physical sciences and arts administration (director of the Poetry Society of America from 1985 to 1988). Mona Van Duyn chose her first book, *The Weight of Numbers*, for the Walt Whitman Prize of the Academy of American Poets. Baumel has also received a grant from the New York Foundation for the Arts. Her second book of poems, *Now*, was published in 1996. She is currently completing a book of translations of the Italian poet Patrizia Cavalli, and her third book of poems, *Blue Branching*, will be published in 2000. She is associate professor of English at Adelphi University and senior lecturer in poetry in the Graduate Program in Creative Writing at City College, New York. She lives in the Bronx with her two sons. She read at KGB on May 12, 1997.

SNOW-DAY

What was it drove me to insist on sleds,
to pull the children out of the playground
and toward the park's much steeper hills, instead
of making angels? I was waist deep and bound
by ice, and they were too. In their eyelashes
was unremovable ice. They crawled and flailed
on snow. The progress of their grudging limbs
slow. Surely memory of snow-fort caches,

the childish city happily derailed,
its hopes of milk and bread and papers dim.

When I was young I came to Boston late
late late one winter night from Baltimore.
The pre-dawn, post-blizzard of seventy-eight
glowed in the silent town where dump trucks bore
their loads of snow as through a secret city—
filling and then dumping in the harbor,
filling yet again. I'd just removed
a child from my womb. Well someone else did it
and it was not a child but some small scar
inside. It meant nothing to me, that newt,

that early fetus, and the procedure meant
nothing except perhaps the end of fear
and queasiness. Today how I resent
the way sadness and loss are souvenirs
we're forced to carry with us. Listen—Happy
is the way I felt, and still I feel,
when I can shovel through the euphemisms
of those who speak for me. More happy. Happy
that forever will that speck, that organism
remain forever small and unfulfilled

in contrast to my son who came exactly
ten years after to the day, and to
a woman ready for him. I had wept

returning to my now-lost lover anew,
seeing the streets of Boston being cleaned,
scraped clear of the invading snow
that clung to arteries, that fairly smothered
our chance to try to make a normal flow
of life. That struggle with the midnight gleam:
the wiping, tidying gesture of a mother.

Gorgeously dramatic Anne Sexton filled Sanders Theater my freshman year at Radcliffe, and the next year, after Sexton had killed herself, Maxine Kumin filled a huge space in Leverett House, wearing, as we would learn, her friend's clothes. Stephen Spender in Science Center B seemed so British and boring we assumed he was too drunk to care. Philip Levine came to the auditorium of Hilles Library and spent most of his interpoem banter talking about Bill Merwin's looks. I was happily appalled by all of them. Greedy for more. Each reading was a gift in those days. We—the student literati—pretended to a *vie bohème*. The Harvard *Advocate* magazine couldn't afford to heat its building; upstairs, Gerard Malanga shivered in his leather jacket so violently his teeth chattered. Mary Jo Salter offered him her gloves. He didn't accept. And the next year I picked Michael Benedikt up from Bay State Road in a taxi the *Advocate* couldn't really afford and found him the cheapest dinner we could. It was at Grendel's Den, which had no liquor license. But he desperately needed a drink. So I scrounged through my purse and got enough coins together for a beer. We stopped at a bar on the way to the reading. I was so nervous I spilled the beer all over him. He saw my face and he saw the situation. He bought his own replacement beer. Later, as director of the Poetry Society of America, I often revisited that humiliation: the first lesson of my life in Po-biz.

JUDITH BAUMEL

"Please indicate by clapping whether you think KGB stands for Kiss Good-bye, for Kant Gooses Bach, for Kitchen Garden Basement, or for Kryptonite's Gay Brother . . ."

"You were marvelous": Poet and Groundwater Press publisher Rosanne Wasserman congratulates her author, Boston-based Ed Barrett, on becoming the second poet ever to use the word haruspicate successfully in a poem. Denis Woychuk (center) approves.

Erin Belieu

Erin Belieu is a visiting assistant professor of English at Kenyon College. Her first book, *Infanta*, was selected for the National Poetry Series and published by Copper Canyon Press. Poems from her new manuscript, *One Above and One Below*, have appeared recently in *Tri Quarterly*, *The Kenyon Review*, and *Boulevard*. In an earlier incarnation, Belieu was a competitive springboard diver, and she has a number of large trophies stashed in her basement. She read at KGB on May 18, 1998.

YOUR CHARACTER IS YOUR DESTINY

but I'm driving:
to where the prairie sulks
like an ex-husband, pissing
away his downtime in a day-old
shave, the permanent arrangement
this sky moved out on years ago.

You're in my jurisdiction,
the territory that makes old men
look older than their unpolished boots;
where only truckers get by, cranked
on speedballs and shooting up what passes
for an incline; where dead-eyed ranch
dogs drink oil from a roadside pool,

sick in the kind of viscous heat that will
fuck you without asking, and

whenever it feels the need.
You're straight out of my town's
post office, not the face on
the flyer but the blank propped up
behind him. You're the new stoplight,

the red direction from nowhere,
the unnecessary signal I want to run.

My most embarrassing moment involved an inexpertly wrapped wrap-around skirt that went dashing to the ground halfway through a reading I once gave at an all-boys prep school in Omaha (and thank God for the podium!). The moral to this story is, of course, that one should always wear her nicest underpants when giving any sort of public performance.

ERIN BELIEU

Erin Belieu reading her poems "Erections," "The Problem of Fidelity," and "The Death of Humphrey Bogart" at KGB.

April Bernard

April Bernard is the author of two books of poems—*Blackbird Bye Bye* and *Psalms*—and a novel, *Pirate Jenny*. She is at work on a book of essays and a third collection of poems. She read at KGB on February 10, 1997.

SEE IT DOES RISE

See it does rise, and will not be stalled
by the dew-point, how murky the aura, nor by the sight
of the face that has been my face, wry-turned on the shelf.
Where does it go to? It goes to the sky
which is also the sea, salted and horse-tailed
and urging toward autumn and its talent to gel
and turn all runny edges to smooth gem-cut sheen.
Straight from my sun the light shoots up,
through my hair, ecstatic, and on to the place
of all light and sharp cider, the taste of apples
pressed free, done with the bark and the bees
and the barrels: the clear golden blood you can pour
on your tongue or on the ground, it has risen past care.

I was invited to Corpus Christi, Texas, to read at an outdoor festival. They set me up in a small tent, with a mike and a few chairs—maybe ten people in the audience. One man in a ten-gallon plastic hat stood at the entrance, chewing on a smoked turkey leg. Two poems in, I was drowned out by extraordinary full-throttle screams from the next tent: the pig races.

APRIL BERNARD

Frank Bidart

Frank Bidart was born in Bakersfield, California, in 1939, and was educated at the University of California, Riverside, and Harvard University. *Desire*, his most recent book of poems, was published in 1997 by Farrar, Straus and Giroux and was short-listed for both the National Book Award and the National Book Critics Circle Award. He has received awards from the Lila Wallace–Reader's Digest Fund and from the American Academy of Arts and Letters. He teaches at Wellesley College and lives in Cambridge, Massachusetts. He read his long poem "The Second Hour of the Night" at KGB on November 3, 1997.

FOR THE TWENTIETH CENTURY

Bound, hungry to pluck again from the thousand
technologies of ecstasy

boundlessness, the world that at a drop of water
rises without boundaries,

I push the PLAY button: —

. . . *Callas, Laurel & Hardy, Szigeti*

you are alive again, —

the slow movement of K. 218
once again no longer

bland, merely pretty, nearly
banal, as it is

in all but Szigeti's hands

***

Therefore you and I and Mozart
must thank the Twentieth Century, for

it made you pattern, form
whose infinite

repeatability within matter
defies matter—

*Malibran. Henry Irving. The young
Joachim* They are lost, a mountain of

newspaper clippings, become words
not their own words. The art of the performer.

Walid Bitar

Walid Bitar was born in Beirut, Lebanon, in 1961. *Two Guys on Holy Land*, a collection of his poems, was published by Wesleyan University Press in 1993. He read at KGB on May 4, 1998.

HAPPY HOUR

I'd 20/20 the dogs
of my august bloodstream,
but my liver can't see:
what it does to liquor
isn't quite what my cornea
does to the world.
And so there's no dousing
my liver with the vistas
I keep strictly visual
to preserve them better,
as if jarred, refrigerated
in my ice sockets
where, like martinis,
they never quite freeze,
where the present, unattached,
like some defective retina,
demands the surgery
of the hands of a clock.

A camera crew from MSNBC wandered into the bar a few minutes before Walid Bitar (left, with poet and critic Albert Mobilio) mounted the podium in May 1998. Walid read "Russian Roulette" ("I live in a dice:/on the ceiling are 6/dot-windows,/on the floor 1,/on the walls/the numbers in between—/a room with 21 views").

Downtown poet and performance artist Eve Packer (right) and Sarah Arvio listen to Donald Hall read his "To a Waterfowl," which has the arresting image of "women with hats like the rear ends of pink ducks."

Star Black

Star Black, codirector of the KGB poetry series, was born in Coronado, California, and was raised in Hawaii and Washington, D.C. She studied English and art history at Wellesley College and became a professional photographer in 1974. She is the author of three books of poetry: *Double Time* (1995; a collection of double sestinas), *Waterworn* (1995), and *October for Idas* (1997). A book of sonnets entitled *Balefire*—the word denoting "a signal fire seen from a distance"—was released by Painted Leaf Press in 1999. She received a poetry grant from the New York Foundation for the Arts in 1997. Her collages have been shown at various galleries in New York and on Long Island. She read at KGB on April 27, 1998.

FROM *BALEFIRE*

RILKE'S LETTER FROM ROME

Certainly you've missed this on your reading list,
or have you? do you truly agree with Rilke's dark
equality, that women should be set free to be who
they are? are you that committed to this anguished

apartness? after all, we're no longer young, hello?
The phone's ringing once again, Housman calling,
the cherry blossoms fall. Frost, hunched upon
the old farm, is gazing at white spiders. Jarrell

is gone, his love for Mary—"Change me, change me"—
is all that is left of him, his beloved semesters,
his street crossings, his crooning essays, and, yes,
each woman misses him as I miss you, immediately,

so, let the letter from Rome go. You've read it. I've
read it. It's a good letter. Not as good as you, though.

TO A WAR CORRESPONDENT

I am here, and shells are quaking over the cracked city,
taking, randomly, its besieged citizenry, one by two by
three, as they, ripped by shrapnel, enter swift mounds
crowding the rubble. I am here, among "fair trails" and

sea salt, thinking of you amidst burials and howitzers,
and how, when you return, there will be only small talk,
strange T.V. channels, vapid parties, and how you will see
everyone scrambling in weird, uninviting careers that

mean nothing pertinent to honor or belief but seem
like flaxen fish aswim within a turquoise aquarium,
quirky and mesmerizing to those who have time for
them, and how the social pages will appear so crazy,

sports events so distant, how you'll pray to be swept
back, out of irrelevance, to hell's urgent significance.

LUST

The Sphinx slinks above the blond commotion
of dust, her eyes disinterested stone, afloat, starkly.
She, too, will reach the jibbed rock's velocity,
its rising throb. She was created for her death —

defeat by mammal, the mammal's swollen feet.
She was created for her trick, its cleaving question.
Man and beast meet in the riddle, daunted, doomed.
She is monstrous on her thriving perch.

Her ears hurt: "Solve me or die, warrior of Thebes.
I am Nietzschean. I am destiny." In a matter of minutes,
she was gone, a simple Simon hurled toward stone,
a lioness exposed in emperor's clothes, easy,

until Nietzsche reversed the roles, and cleaving
armies attained the claw's perch: no more one-to-one.

THE BLANK ABANDON OF BEDS

Esperance! The twinge of moonlight in outer space,
its circulating tea cups of planets, the floury face
no longer inscrutable in a half-frown but full and
voluble, agape. We are about to land upon a nostril.

There are no hulas here, simply dissolving patter
on silver silt in gravity's void, our heads abubble

with the merest molecules aswirl within. Our Velcro
fingers web and clench, we hover upon the lonely

homestead, its unembarrassed crude silhouette,
its entombing gradients. See the silt's dissolution
of nationalities, how every booted imprint fits,
how clean this map is, without Clio's grievances.

We've made it. Science has hurled our hearts far,
mashed in Velcro, yet we are two; our hands hold.

PERSONALS

Approximate and unfulfilled, a devilish nymph
in the underworld seeks huge black swan for fiery
twills in cranium's caverns, gray-matter indifference
preferred, although will take sensitivity, as well,

if inexperience in hell is available, for long-term
committed one-flight stand with ensuing consequences
such as bestial transformations and showering soot.
Nymph will attempt to run, as required, from

dark thwunking destiny. Nymph will not be easy
to acquire, though promised to succumb to aerial fury.
Various disguises necessary, drop chute appreciated.

Do not send photograph, please; visuals confusing,
element of surprise essential, fact of advertisement
accidental. Pretend you don't read and never will.

HOOPLA

You've aroused the lilacs and they brew violets
with inappropriate fluidity. You could have laid
upon the posies, quietly, and not breathed, dewly,
into purplish hollows, evoked the virtual from

sequential flowers, the sky above: the cellophane
of love. You could have scuffed peat moss, worn
canvas gloves, mowed and mowed, and not become
Ferdinand in the *fleur's* blur. You could've claimed

the entourage of grass in the blistery sun, flimsy
trowels dirty; trundled upon larvae on explicit
lawns, instead of yawning like a bored bull. Hmm,
a purple minotaur, well, I've seen them before

although heroics were less listless back when,
yet chivalry adjusts. You never know about men.

Robert Bly

Robert Bly was born in Madison, Minnesota, in 1926. His most recent collection of poems, *Morning Poems*, is out in paperback from Harper-Collins. He edited for Ecco Press an anthology of spiritual poems called *The Soul Is Here for Its Own Joy: Sacred Poems from Many Cultures*. He is the author of *The Sibling Society* (Vintage) and, with Marion Woodman, *The Maiden King: The Reunion of Masculine and Feminine* (Holt). He was guest editor of *The Best American Poetry 1999*. He read at KGB on March 26, 1998.

THE DAY WE VISITED NEW ORLEANS

So much time has gone by! Napoleon's house—
He never came—still stands in the Quarter.
Time erases all the good living that Louis
The Sixteenth, after the decapitation, never
Experienced, all the sights Andrew
Jackson never saw in Pirate's Alley.
Ask the alligators about heat and history.

Out in the bayous we met a small alligator
Named Elvis. When we stroked his throat, he waved
His left claw at the world. It makes you think.
Alligators enjoy a world before the alphabet.

I don't want to be who you are! I want
To be who I am, someone playing with language.

Let us each be a sensualist
Of the imponderable! Let's each do
What we want. I thread my way
Down alphabets to the place where Elvis is.

*Robert Bly extends the outstretched arm of male friendship, while
painter Judith Vivell and poet Kambiz Naficy applaud.*

One gets used to unexpected situations after a while. A large university in
Cleveland, which had really a daytime campus, decided to try a poetry
reading at night and invited me for that night. When I arrived, I found an
old-fashioned hall with about five hundred of those wooden theater seats
made of curved black wood and four people sitting in the front row. One
was a teacher who kept looking anxiously over her shoulder, looking for
floods of students to pour in, who never did. During my early years as a
reader, I would have read to the whole empty hall miserably. We would all
have gone out depressed. This time I said, "Does anyone have an apart-
ment near here?" It turned out someone did, and we had a wonderful read-
ing in a small room with a sofa. A reading requires human interflow, and
it's worth walking a few blocks to get it.

ROBERT BLY

Tom Breidenbach

Tom Breidenbach lives in New York City. His poems have appeared in the *Denver Quarterly*, *College English*, *American Poetry Review*, the *Mississippi Review*, and *Lingo*. He read at KGB on March 10, 1997.

CONFESSIONAL

"I'm the naked power-grab!" yodel the latecomers.
"Me the walled nobody of a circus clown," sputters one smudge,
"glue to the nose of a bad child!"
"I put the rampage at a tissue door," volunteers the razzle-dazzle.
"We are the injured nursing these flaws our life in oblivion," wagers the
    peacemaker.
"I've the cure," antes the decapitant.
"Me, me, the discharge of a slain halfwit dribbled to a rut!"
"Me, me, rage for smut cramping the orphan's lap!"
Each choruses, "we welcome the wash of this doom against us
with the perpetual distances it shall multiply in our steads
and the fever of these salutes charges the blossom of our impasse!"

*Tom Breidenbach (left) moved to New York City via Massachusetts from a
farming community in northeastern Colorado. Here with his
photographer pal Iannis Delatolas.*

*Gyorgyi Voros (right) drove up from Virginia to read for an audience that
included her mentor, Judith Gleason, Parnassus contributor and an
anthologist of African poetry.*

Tom Carey

Tom Carey was born in Santa Monica, California, the scion of two generations of cowboy actors. He studied acting with Jack Garfein and Stella Adler, appearing in films such as *Plaza Suite* and *The Day of the Locust*. In 1977 he moved to New York, where he sang, acted, wrote, and finally, in 1988, became a Franciscan brother in the Society of St. Francis, a religious order in the Episcopal Church. He currently lives and works in Brooklyn, New York. He read at KGB on March 23, 1998.

ZOHAR

For Jane DeLynn

I keep meaning to tell you
about the thirteen mystics
expelled from Spain
by the demonic Isabella,
how they knew the secret
of binding words to air.
And when light poured
like oil
over the head of Aaron,
they saw love,
indifference and need,
objects speeding through time,
low speaking clouds.
So, someone cuts
and someone eats,
and someone always remembers
the agony and grace.

A five-year-old
running into the spray,
falls over a wagon.
Now this is the question:
The boy wailing
into the daichondra,
droplets cupped in green
and the sun in them.
The thirteen exiles stood,
their backs touching
a wall in Safed,
and they watched
while one ate bread
and knew it mattered more
than they knew.
One elbow's on the table
the knife's
on the kitchen counter.
Neurons never actually touching
remember Second Avenue.
If it was, never was,
don't matter.
Everything's a mess.
Something speaks
in the arrangements.

I have a version of the "actor's dream." About every six or eight months I dream that I'm in a large auditorium—someplace big, like the Ninety-second Street Y or even Town Hall. I'm there to read my poems, I'm anxious. Everyone is here: my parents, all my closest friends; even the dead are here: Jimmy Schuyler; my brother, Steve; Tim Dlugos; both my grandmothers. I'm backstage waiting to go on. I can see the bright lights of the stage area. John Wayne is out there gesturing and laughing, and the crowd is applauding. I look down at my hands to see what they're holding. They're not holding anything! I have no poems! I frantically scan the area around me to see where I could have dropped them. Nothing. I start running around. I speak to anyone who will listen—I've lost my poems. I tell Eileen Myles, who says that I must have left them in Mexico. I'm momentarily distracted by a beautiful youth who takes my hand, gives me an inviting smile, and asks me if I'm reading this evening. Yes, I say. No! I can't find my poems! I try to remember some of them, maybe I can recite a few. But I'm hopelessly tied to the page, I can only remember bits. It's time. I have to go on. I walk out onstage, under the lights, stand at a microphone, and begin making my poems up as I go along.

TOM CAREY

Tom Carey worked as the late James Schuyler's assistant. Schuyler's poem "Tom" concludes with a salute to "Thomas Paul Carey of/ Sherman Oaks, California,/who writes and sings/his own rock songs, the/son and grandson of two/great movie actors, the/two Harry Careys."

Marc Cohen

Marc Cohen was born in Brooklyn in 1951. His two books of poems, both from Groundwater Press, are *On Maplewood Time* (1988) and *Mecox Road* (1997). His work has also appeared in three volumes of *The Best American Poetry*. He splits his time between New York City and Sag Harbor, Long Island. He read at KGB on December 15, 1997.

EVENSONG

Being alone is the next best thing
to being with her   Fleet skeletons of music
dance on fallen leaves   Silver birches
bathe in pools of afternoon sun
Amid the confusion
of spring dispersals
a misguided bird cracks
the shell of a crooked day

The music stops
Darkness coats the ugly day
sheds light
on the only way
to break the solitude

lay down beside her again

Marc Cohen read "Psyche Said" at KGB. The poem concludes, "Just before Psyche disappeared / behind the thunderclouds, / you could hear the raindrops whisper / that Eros had lost his clout. / Then the train left the station."

Billy Collins

Billy Collins's latest collection is *Picnic, Lightning* (University of Pittsburgh Press, 1998). His National Poetry Series collection, *Questions About Angels*, was reissued by Pittsburgh in the spring of 1999. He teaches at Lehman College (CUNY) and Sarah Lawrence College. He read at KGB on April 7, 1997.

TOMES

There is a section in my library for death
and another for Irish history,
a few shelves for the poetry of China and Japan,
and in the center a row of imperturbable reference books,
the ones you can turn to anytime,
when the night is going wrong
or when the day is full of empty promise.

I have nothing against
the thin monograph, the odd query,
a note on the identity of Chekhov's dentist,
but what I prefer on days like these
is to get up from the couch,
pull down *The History of the World,*
and hold in my hands a book
containing nearly everything
and weighing no more than a sack of potatoes,
11 pounds, I discovered one day when I placed it

on the black, iron scale
my mother used to keep in her kitchen,
the device on which she would place
a certain amount of flour,
a certain amount of fish.

Open flat on my lap
under a halo of lamplight,
a book like this always has a way
of soothing the nerves,
quieting the riotous surf of information
that foams around my waist
even though it never mentions
the silent labors of the poor,
the daydreams of grocers and tailors,
or the faces of men and women alone in single rooms—
even though it never mentions my mother,
now that I think of her again,
who only last year rolled off the edge of the earth
in her electric bed,
in her smooth pink nightgown,
the bones of her fingers interlocked,
her sunken eyes staring upward
beyond all knowledge,
beyond the tiny figures of history,
some in uniform, some not,
marching onto the pages of this incredibly heavy book.

Here's a story that contains probably the best and worst experiences I have had in connection with poetry readings.

A couple of years ago, a woman named Jackie telephoned me from southern Florida with the most exotic reading invitation I had ever received. She wanted to know if I would be interested in coming to Palm Beach for a week in February to give five readings, each at a different branch of a large, private, Chicago-based bank. That's *bank* as in where they keep the money. Every branch apparently had its own "literary society," which convened a couple of times a year for a literary luncheon complete with live author. It was a smart public relations idea considering that there was a long waiting list to join at every branch. The rich were kept happily entertained, and the honorable ties between literature and money were strengthened. Jackie told me that their list of past authors included best-selling favorites such as Antonia Fraser and Cleveland Amory. I would be their first poet. She named a hefty honorarium. Plus the bank would purchase eight hundred copies of my new book and distribute them to all the members. Bookplates would be mailed to me to be signed. Wagging my tail, I accepted.

February finally rolled around, and one day, around lunchtime, exactly a week before the date of the first reading, the phone rang at home. It was Jackie. She seemed stunned that I had answered. "What's the matter?" I asked her. "You're supposed to be here in Florida *today, now!*" The airhead poet had made plane reservations for the following week. Just seven days off. Seventeen hundred miles to the south, a roomful of people were waiting for me to make my entrance. Hyperventilating, I asked if I could call her back in five minutes, then I hung up the phone and paced around the house emitting tiny sounds I had not made since infancy. You have to understand that this is the stuff of all my nightmares. I am hopelessly late for some performance. I am lost in a maze of corridors looking for the auditorium. I step up to the podium and it shatters. I open my book to read and the pages are blank or covered with Cyrillic letters. Here I was in the middle of a real-life bad dream.

I felt like crawling naked down the interstate from New York to Florida as a token of my abjectitude, but when I called back, full of apology, Jackie, cool and gracious, said she would do some "damage control" and the readings could be rescheduled for May if that was all right with me.

The tour itself was as delightful as I had imagined. I was put up for a week in a small, luxurious, British-run Palm Beach hotel with a lively bar scene at night. Every morning at eleven, a chauffeur would pick me up and drive me to a heavily marbled bank in places like Boca Raton and Delray Beach. I would be ushered into a large meeting room set for lunch and crowded with the most beautiful elderly women I have ever seen, all dressed up in brightly colored Chanel suits. I would sit at the head table and answer questions about this-and-that while I pushed my lobster salad around on my plate and wondered about the net worth of all the people at the table. Then I would get up and read my poems to polite applause. I don't know how many of the women actually read my book, but they all seemed happy for the chance to get out of the house. Many came up and said how much they enjoyed my "speech." The few men at the luncheons looked extremely tired, and I guessed that some of the wives were afraid their husbands might start playing with the stove if left alone at home. After every reading, the driver would return me to the hotel, and I would have the rest of the afternoon (laps in the pool, nap) and night (dinner at my usual table, then drinks at the bar) to myself.

The sixth day, on the way back to the airport, I asked the driver—we were pals by now—to put on the local jazz station. Then I sank back into the soft leather of the backseat and watched the palm trees slide by. "Surely," I thought to myself, "poetry can make *something* happen."

BILLY COLLINS

John Yau continues the noble lineage of poets who work as art critics. Under the title Please Wait by the Coatroom, he is gathering recent essays on poets (such as Walt Whitman, Hart Crane, Weldon Kees, Frank O'Hara) and painters (including Jean-Michel Basquiat, Joseph Stella, Jess, Bruce Nauman). The University of Michigan Press will publish it.

Anne Porter (right) published her first book of poems when she was eighty-four. It was promptly shortlisted for the National Book Award in poetry. Porter's late husband, Fairfield, painted a striking portrait of poet Ron Padgett (left) in 1970.

Douglas Crase

Douglas Crase was born in 1944 in Battle Creek, Michigan. He dropped out of law school to write for the political reform commission of the Michigan Democratic Party. For thirteen years he wrote speeches for corporate clients including Eastman Kodak, General Electric, United Technologies, and ITT. His sole book of poems so far, *The Revisionist*, was published by Little, Brown in 1981, listed as a Notable Book of the Year by *The New York Times*, and nominated for the National Book Critics Circle Award and the American Book Award. It also earned the Witter Bynner Prize from the American Academy and Institute of Arts and Letters. The critic David Kalstone said it appeared "with that sense of completion of utterance and of identity that must have come with the first books of Wallace Stevens and Elizabeth Bishop." Another critic compared it to early Miles Davis instead. Crase wrote the introduction to the Vintage/Library of America paperback of Emerson's *Essays*, and his unusual commonplace book, *AMERIFIL. TXT*, has been published by the University of Michigan Press. He has received a Guggenheim Fellowship, a Whiting Writers Award, and a MacArthur Fellowship for his poems and essays. He lives in New York and in Carley Brook, Pennsylvania. He read "Astropastoral" at KGB on October 6, 1997. It is printed here for the first time.

ASTROPASTORAL

As much as the image of you, I have seen
You again, live, as in live indecision you brighten
The limbs of an earth that so earnestly turns

To reflect you, the sky's brightest body
And last best beacon for those who are everywhere
Coded in spirals and want to unbend,
Who bear in the dark turned toward you
This message they have to deliver even to live,
To linger in real time before you, to meet or to
Blow you away—and yes I have seen you receive them
But you are not there. Though I've tried to ignore you,
Go solo, light out beyond you,
I have seen you on every horizon, how you are stored
And encouraged and brought to the brim
Until the round bounds of one planet could not hold you in
But were ready to set near space ringing
As if from the ranking capacitor outside the sun.
I have seen you discharged, and then how you swell
Toward heaven and how you return, transmitting the fun
Of the firmament, all of it yours. And these things
Have happened, only you are not there.
At night in the opposite high-rise I'd see how you glow,
And in the adjacent one too, the same would-be blue,
And I've looked on the glow in the waters
Around the reactor, that also blue, how
Whatever would match your expression you
Wouldn't be there. I have seen the impressions you leave
At the margin of error in exit polls, monitored polls
That you never entered—I can tell what I see:
Saw you vote with your feet and hit the ground running,
Kiss the ground, rescued, and (this wasn't a drill)
Saw you fall to your knees on the ground

By the body of your friend on the ground
And though these fall beside you like gantries, it is
You who are rising above them and you are not there.
Like a rocket in winter, I have been there to see you
Logged in as a guest among stars—only you,
Though you're lovely to look at, expensive to own,
And though in demand without letup, you are not there.

The truth is I don't remember the words of a single poem from a single poetry reading. There were the words of Vachel Lindsay, boomlay boom, recited to a hall of sophomores. But that is a memory impelled by embarrassment, and besides it wasn't the lecturer's poem. There was the debut of Ashbery's double-columned "Litany," but that is a memory of the two readers required to read it. The poems whose actual words I do remember are those I read silently myself in bed. Why get out of bed and go to a reading? Sometimes there is a party afterward. This I discovered at the first reading I attended on my own, in a small college town, from the helpful professor who said there is a party afterward but I can't take you because you are uninvited. It is a joy to come to New York and go where you are uninvited. Then after the party who can remember the poems? I recall in detail the one true benchmark reading in my life, no boomlay boomlay, but uninflected, like the scrim of smoke from the poet's Gauloises. The scales fell from my ears. The detail I do not recall is a single word. Surely the most historic reading was a practice session for James Schuyler prior to his first big public appearance. I remember the apartment on Ninth Street, who was there, and that we were not so historic after all. An A-team had assembled for an earlier run. Clearest in retrospect is the indivisible authority with which, as he read, the "shy" poet inhabited his poems. I could not tell you which poems they were. In sum you might say that the readings eclipse the poems, just as the cynical say they do, and the only reason to get yourself combed and out to a reading is fear of death. Yet poetry was forever altered by these readings whose words I remember not at all. There is an explanation, though it is perhaps not a fashionable one. It was formulated in a way I like by Wallace Stevens. Poetry is ("almost incredibly," he said) an effect of analogy, and a poet's controlling analogy is a sense of the world. But what if his sense of the world is that it's clubbable? Or hers that it's redeemed by her appreciating glance? What if, as you are entitled to hope, his or her sense of the world is alien as experience itself? This is poetics poetry can't deny. At readings whose words will randomize into air, it may be unforgettably on display.

DOUGLAS CRASE

Douglas Crase has a reputation among poets as a world-class recluse, but you wouldn't know it from his frequent sightings at KGB.

Carl Dennis

Carl Dennis teaches in the English department at the State University of New York, Buffalo, and at Warren Wilson College. He has published seven books of poetry, most recently *Ranking the Wishes* (Penguin, 1997). The poem included here, originally published in *Poetry*, is from a newly completed manuscript called *Practical Gods*. He read at KGB on February 23, 1998.

ST. FRANCIS AND THE NUN

The message St. Francis preached to the birds,
Though not recorded, isn't beyond surmising.
He wanted his fellow creatures to taste the joy
Of singing not only to please each other
But to praise creation, to offer hymns of thanksgiving
Similar to the hymns he sang on waking.
Granted the birds had little talent for language,
But maybe they'd grasp enough of his earnest tone
To feel that spring shouldn't be taken lightly.
An audience hard to hold, to be sure,
With a narrow attention span, a constant fluttering,
But a lot less challenging than the nun he counseled
Only this morning, a woman still young
Dying slowly in pain, who asked him
Why if her suffering had a purpose
That purpose couldn't be clarified in a vision.
Why not at least some evidence

That the greater the suffering reserved for her
The smaller the portion reserved for others?
What a balm to be able to think as Jesus did,
That with every difficult breath of hers
Patients in sick beds around the world
Suddenly found they were breathing easier.
What a relief for St. Francis these birds are,
Free of the craving for explanation, for certainty
Even in winter, when the grass is hidden. "Look!"
He calls to them, pointing. "Those black specks
There in the snow are seed husks. Think
As you circle down how blessed you are."
But what can he point to in the nun's spare cell
To keep her from wondering why it's so hard
For the king of heaven to comfort her?
All she can manage now is to hope for the will
Not to abandon her god, if he is her god,
In his hour of weakness. No time to reply
To the tender homily at her bedside
As she gathers all her strength for the end,
Hoping to cry out briefly as Jesus did
When his body told him he was on his own.

Tom Disch

Tom Disch was born in Des Moines, Iowa, in 1940 and was raised in Minnesota. His most recent collections of poems are *Dark Verses and Light* (Johns Hopkins University Press, 1991) and *A Child's Garden of Grammar* (University Press of New England, 1997). His most recent novel is *The Priest: A Gothic Romance* (Knopf, 1995). His collection of poetry criticism, *The Castle of Indolence* (Picador, 1995), was nominated for the National Book Critics Circle Award in criticism. He is a drama critic for the New York *Daily News*. He read at KGB on December 8, 1997.

THE AGREEMENT OF PREDICATE PRONOUNS

"If you were me . . ." the lad began.
"But that can't be, my little man,

You must be I with verbs like were."
He heaved a sigh. "If I were *her* . . ."

"Then you'd be *she*. Let me explain:
The verb to be—" "You're such a pain!

Suppose I said that I were *you?*"
"Then you'd be I, and that would do."

"But you're just who I would not be."
"That may be true, but we'd agree,

And that is what pronouns must do.
You're *not* me. But—I could be you."

Among the many elements of the twentieth century that postmodern children can only puzzle over—things like pumps and privies—the intricacies of English grammar still have, for me, the commemorative power of Vicks VapoRub. In fifth and sixth grades I enjoyed diagramming sentences better than recess. Grammar, I firmly believe, can be even more fun than algebra!

For those who feel a similar nostalgia for the distinctions between transitive and intransitive verbs, as well as for those who've never learned the difference between *lie* and *lay*, I wrote *A Child's Garden of Grammar*. Shortly after it was brought out by the University Press of New England in 1997, I read the whole book aloud at my KGB reading, and Sister Fidelis looked down beaming from her blackboard in the sky.

TOM DISCH

Tom Disch (right) wants Anne Lehman to tell him about her son David's mischievous childhood.

Denise Duhamel

Denise Duhamel was born in 1961 in Providence, Rhode Island, and was educated at Sarah Lawrence College (M.F.A.) and Emerson College (B.F.A.). *The Star-Spangled Banner* (Southern Illinois University Press, winner of the Crab Orchard Poetry Prize) was published in 1999. Her other poetry books include *Exquisite Politics* (a collaborative volume with Maureen Seaton, Tia Chucha Press, 1997), *Kinky* (Orchises Press, 1997), *How the Sky Fell* (Pearl Editions, 1996), *Girl Soldier* (Garden Street Press, 1995), and *The Woman with Two Vaginas* (Salmon Run Press, 1995). She has been awarded grants from the Ludwig Vogelstein Foundation, the Puffin Foundation, and the New York Foundation for the Arts. She lives with her husband, the poet Nick Carbó, in New York City. She read at KGB on March 31, 1997.

SEX WITH A FAMOUS POET

I had sex with a famous poet last night
and when I woke up beside him I shuddered
because I was married to someone else,
because I wasn't supposed to have been drinking,
because I was in a car from the fifties
wearing a dress from the fifties
parked on a dirt road I didn't recognize
and the famous poet was drooling,
boxes of his books between us. I would have told you
right off this was a dream, but recently
a friend told me, *write about a dream,*

lose a reader, and I didn't want to lose you
right away. I wanted you to hear
that I didn't even like the poet in the dream, that he has
four kids, the youngest one my age, and I find him
rather unattractive, that I met him only once,
that is, in real life, and that was in a large group
in which I barely spoke up. He disgusted me
with his disparaging remarks about women.
He even used the word "Jap"
which I took as a direct insult to my husband who's Asian.
In the dream I guessed he'd given a reading—
because of the box of books—where maybe I met him,
where maybe I hung around like a groupie
to drink the free wine and flirt a little,
where maybe I didn't tell him I was a poet myself
or maybe I did, hoping he could help my career.
I don't remember anything before the car,
and the vague sensation of having had sex
the night before. When we were first dating
I told the man who became my husband,
"You were talking in your sleep last night
And I listened, just to make sure you didn't
call out anyone else's name." My husband said
that he couldn't be held responsible for his subconscious
which worried me, which made me think his dreams
were full of blond vixens in rabbit-fur bikinis,
but he said no, he dreamt mostly about boulders
and the ocean and volcanoes, dangerous weather
he witnessed but could do nothing about to stop.

And I said, "I dream only of you,"
which was romantic and silly and untrue.
But I never thought I'd dream of another man—
my husband and I hadn't even had a fight,
my head tucked sweetly in his armpit, my arm
around his belly which lifted up and down
all night, gently like water in a lake.
There were a lot of books in that box
which makes me think maybe the famous poet
didn't sell many at his reading, which was my way
of insulting him in my dream, since I created
the whole thing. Maybe it was the fifties
because of the poet's antiquated views of women
and the Japanese. It was right after World War II
and women were back in their kitchens,
everyone still reeling about the atrocities.
I've also read that everyone in your dreams is you,
or at least an aspect of your personality,
in which case maybe the famous poet is someone
I want to integrate with and become.
My therapist says there were at least three kinds
of dreams—the kind in which you're working
something out, the kind that suggest a premonition,
and the kind that are junk, the mind churning
and shredding, the mind simply a compost.
So all I can do is hope my dream was the junk kind
and the poet I dreamt about has forgotten me completely,
that if I met him on the street or at a conference
he would walk by, famous in his sunglasses

or blazer with the suede patches at the elbows,
without so much as a glance in my direction.
I know you're probably curious about who the poet is,
so I should tell you the clues I've left aren't completely
accurate, that I've pretty much disguised his identity,
that you shouldn't guess *I bet it's him* . . .
because you'll never guess correctly
and if you do, I won't tell you that you have.
I wouldn't want to embarrass a stranger
who is, after all, probably a nice person,
whom I probably just met on a bad day,
who probably is growing a little tired of his fame—
which my husband and I perceive as enormous,
but how much fame can an American poet
really have, let's say, compared to a rock star
or film director of equal talent? Not that much,
and the famous poet knows it, knows that he's not
truly given his due. Knows that many
of these young poets tugging on his sleeve
are only pretending to have read all his books.
But he smiles anyway, tries to be helpful.
I mean, this poet has to have some redeeming qualities, right?
For instance, he writes a mean iambic.
Otherwise, what was I doing in his car.

I've always considered myself a pretty lucky gal when it comes to poetry. No one, for example, has ever thrown up during one of my readings. (Not so for the Long Beach poet Gerald Locklin. The vomiter in his audience was sitting in the front row.) I've never heard anyone snore during one of my readings. (But a friend who prefers to remain anonymous confided that during one of her readings in Cambridge, someone got up from his folding chair to lie down in the aisle and take a little snooze. Even more unfortunately, that person was her mentor.)

Sure, there have been the occasional disappointments. Once I showed up to read at a planetarium, a pretty huge one even by planetarium standards, and no one but the organizer and his wife were there. Shortly after my first chapbook came out and I was hawking copies to pay the electric bill, someone slipped a hand into the coat I'd left on the back of a chair while I was onstage and stole all my hard-earned chapbook money right out of my pocket. Another time, in a group reading, I was scheduled to follow a poet who ceremoniously pulled down his pants and swayed his penis as he recited. Not an easy act to follow, and the drunken listeners voiced their disappointment when I hit the stage fully clothed.

I never felt in danger until I judged a slam. I was having fun, giving pretty good scores, until a man recited a poem so vile that I've since managed to block most of it from my memory, except for the fact that it involved a woman's vagina smelling like a dead fish. The vagina he wrote about may have even belonged to his mother, but my memory could be exaggerating. I wrote "no comment" on my score card. This was in the funky loose rule days of the Nuyorican Poets Cafe when people often gave pi or infinity signs as scores. My "no comment" didn't seem out of character. But the host, Bob bless-his-heart Holman, urged me to come up with a number, so I finally chose zero. The poet didn't seem disappointed; maybe he was used to being misunderstood. But when the crowd began their normal fun-loving booing, I detected a more sinister sound from a corner table. The slam went on. Another poet won. I drank a few diet Cokes and danced a bit before leaving. Some young groupies of the poet who hated vaginas circled me on Avenue B. They called me bad names. As they were deciding whether they should beat my head against the sidewalk, I flagged down a cop car, which, luckily for me, was making its rounds.

If I'd had the presence of mind, I would have told those fiercely devoted listeners that they shouldn't have been so upset—all I did was give their favorite poet a goose egg. In the scheme of things, that poet was pretty lucky. No one in the audience shot at him, for example. (Lower East Side folklore had it that someone took out a gun and fired a few bullets at a poet during an open mike in the seventies.) I've never seen that particular group of poetry lovers at a reading since—maybe they sensed how unfair and disappointing the poetry world can sometimes be. Nevertheless, these listeners left their impression on me. Ever since that night, I tend to clap wildly when a fellow poet steps up to the mike.

DENISE DUHAMEL

Denise Duhamel read at KGB a few weeks after the Poet's Theatre gave four performances of her play How the Sky Fell *at St. Mark's Place in March 1997.*

Elaine Equi

Elaine Equi was born in Oak Park, Illinois, in 1953. Her most recent books of poetry, *Decoy* (1994) and *Voice-Over* (1999), were published by Coffee House Press. She lives in New York City and teaches at the New School for Social Research, the Writers Voice, and City College. She read at KGB on March 9, 1998.

AUTOBIOGRAPHICAL POEM

The story of my skin
is long and involved.

While the story of my hair
is quite short.

In the story of my mouth
kisses linger over poppyseeds

and crumbs of lemon-scented cake.
There is a character who always builds

in the story of my bones
and a woman who refuses to leave

her gondola in the story of my blood.
But it is the heart's story

I most want to share
with you who also know this pleasure

of being shut inside
a vast dark place, alone—

as if at a small table
scribbling lies.

One of the most ridiculous things that ever happened to me was when the Museum of Contemporary Art in Chicago called the police because I and another poet, Jerome Sala, were behaving lasciviously during a reading by Robert Creeley (a real favorite of mine, by the way). Mostly, we were just drunk and making out, but being young, and writers ourselves, we were intoxicated not only with vodka but also with the whole idea of poetry, which suddenly seemed glaringly at odds with the museum's sanctimonious atmosphere. After that incident, gossip spread, and people were always on the lookout for us to create some kind of disturbance at literary events. As we were usually drunk, it was easy to comply. People who know me now (as someone who doesn't even smoke) find it hard to believe. But back in the late seventies, I was ejected from more than one reading for my overly enthusiastic audience participation.

ELAINE EQUI

Jonathan Galassi

Jonathan Galassi was born in Seattle in 1949 and grew up in Massachusetts. He studied at Harvard University and Cambridge University. He is editor in chief of Farrar, Straus and Giroux. *Morning Run*, a collection of his poems, was published by Paris Review Editions in 1988. In 1998 Farrar, Straus and Giroux published his translation of Eugenio Montale's *Collected Poems, 1920–1954*. He read at KGB on November 17, 1997.

ARGUMENT

Chaotic sun on asphalt camouflages
the order of the shadows that the trees
throw down in mulled, multivalent mirages:
wheels within wheels—I've had my share of these.

The clouds upstairs, too, seem to move by magic;
their hectic travels never look the same.
I can't see their wildness has a logic
and I don't know my wildness has a name.

I am not by and large a fan of poetry readings—unless I know (and love) the work of the performer. Only then is a reading a not-to-be-missed opportunity to learn how familiar work sounds in the voice of its creator. New work seems hard to absorb.

But my experience of KGB, the bar in New York's East Village where David Lehman and Star Black have been running a Monday night series for the past several years, is almost enough to make me abandon my prejudice. The pre–(Russian) Revolutionary locale—up a set of steep, rickety stairs in a curtained-off, dimly lit, red barroom decorated with old Commie memorabilia—gives the gathering a committed, not to say conspiratorial air and, along with the very good martinis, somehow manages to foster a true sense of camaraderie, experimentation, and open exchange between readers and audience. I've seldom enjoyed an evening of poetry and friendship more. Within KGB's cozy, grimy walls you can almost convince yourself that the fabulous heroic underground New York of O'Hara and Schuyler and Denby, of Ginsberg, Corso, and LeRoi Jones, is still alive and well. If only all such encounters could be so warm and generous and anxiety-free!

JONATHAN GALASSI

*Philip Levine signing books for younger poets David Nielsen
and Amudha Rajendran.*

*Poet and novelist Jaime Manriqué moved to New York City after the
controversial reception of his first novel in his native Colombia.*

Suzanne Gardinier

Suzanne Gardinier was born in New Bedford, Massachusetts, and attended the University of Massachusetts and Columbia University. She is the author of *The New World* (University of Pittsburgh Press, 1993) and *A World That Will Hold All the People* (University of Michigan Press, 1996). She lives in Manhattan and teaches at Sarah Lawrence College. She read at KGB on October 20, 1997.

TWO GIRLS

who come in the night whispering
Whose songs are too small to remember
Whose rest Whose gestures disappeared
To look for them without a sentence
To make a shelter for them here
One night dance One firstlight singer
Who mark each lost nearness with tears
One torn cloth coat One pact unmended
Who warn in whispers fifty years
One who wants the word for morning
Two we think are here no longer
One who wants the word for footprint
Two girls tangled in the branches
One in smoke One in shadow
One from bridges One from snow
Kaddish
The languages of wrists and ankles

Winter Soup Bread A woman's neck

Sealed train to suddenly an island

Here she who lay down her small flesh

This crow This star This metal bramble

This path where craft and bodies mesh

This night chimney This ditch This shamble

To manufacture smoke from breath

What you know of masks Of making

Forest clearing built of ashes

Nachtwache The word for footprint

All the songs you have forgotten

This ghost fury This disguise

Borrowed mouth and borrowed eyes.

at exactly 8:15 a.m. a thousand doves released from cages

Mountain flanks Barley Delta bridges

Salt river's movement in the heat

Summer Daughter Breakfast Two fishes

Shadows The language shadows speak

A cricket Just before the brightness

She who watches She who has seen

Invention heralded by engines

This labor's fruit This planned machine

Straw umbrellas Coats of paper

Temples choked with unclaimed ashes

Thirst *Zensho* The word for morning

She who could not keep her skin on

Nachtwache: nightwatchman

Zensho: conflagration

You who call her No Witness
You who think she found her rest
You
Her hair smoothed back from fever forehead
Her chill in nearness put away
The fledgling kept The sapling guarded
These two who knock with every rain
Where there is warmth Where there is water
The stamping songs of yesterday
Two guardians Two raging daughters
You who were taught another way
You who think a word is useless
You who mock and doubt your dreaming
You who know dirt is not holy
You who never were a child
Archipelago Cistern
You hungry You thirsty Turn

Dana Gioia

Dana Gioia was born in Los Angeles in 1950. He studied at Stanford and Harvard Universities, and now lives in California with his wife and children. He is the author of two books of poems, *Daily Horoscope* (1986) and *The Gods of Winter* (1991), as well as a volume of criticism, *Can Poetry Matter* (1992), all of which were published by Graywolf Press. He has also written an opera libretto, *Nosferatu*, for the composer Alva Henderson. He read at KGB on May 18, 1998.

FAILURE

As with any child, you find your own more beautiful—
eager to nurse it along, watch over it,
and taking special pride as each day
it grows more gorgeously like you.

Why not consider it a sort of accomplishment?
Failure doesn't happen by itself. It takes time,
effort, and a certain undeniable gift.
Satisfaction comes from recognizing what you do best.

Most of what happens is never intended,
but deep inside you know you planned this—
not a slip or a fumble but a total rout.
You only fail at what you really aim for.

Unusual things often happen at poetry readings—some wonderful, some annoying, and some just odd. One evening about ten years ago I arrived at a large and well-appointed Soho loft to give a reading. After greeting me, the organizer introduced me to a beautiful young woman. The reading series, he informed me, had just received a grant to hire an interpreter to sign the poems for "the hearing-impaired members of the audience." (What fun one could have exploring the implications of *that* phrase!) It seemed like a well-meaning but profoundly useless idea—and very American in its conviction that art itself was not worth funding without some uplifting or utilitarian social agenda. Of course, I kept my skepticism to myself. Nowadays no artist dares stand between an arts administrator and his funding. And more important, it seemed ungallant to keep this young lady from getting her paycheck. My "interpreter" asked if she could look at the texts I intended to read. I showed her a few of the poems. "These are hard to do," she said. From the way she held herself I guessed she had been a dancer. I asked and learned that she had indeed been a ballerina. "Don't worry about signing every word or phrase," I said. "You can always dance them a bit to bring across the mood. Interpret." And so she did— signing, swaying, and dancing—a perfect collaborator. As it turned out, there were no deaf or hearing-impaired people in the audience, but you would have had to have been blind not to have enjoyed her choreography.

DANA GIOIA

At KGB, Dana Gioia (right)—pictured here with his son Teddy and with the poet and translator Michael Palma—read his poems "Litany" and "Summer Storm" as well as the vampire's "Nocturne" from his libretto for Alva Henderson's opera Nosferatu.

Heartthrob Eric Minton was our bartender during the raucous first year of the series. ·

Lucy Grealy

Lucy Grealy is the author of a chapbook of poems, *Everyday Alibis*; a memoir, *Autobiography of a Face*; and numerous essays. She is working on a novel and lives in Manhattan. She read at KGB on June 2, 1997.

MURDER

Death was hours ago but already words
have blotted up the last rivulets of trace,
already children sing songs that rhyme
with him on the streets.
No one knows who did it.

In the city's only theater thighs press
between shows, the urging so explosive
it reaches the montage of sparrows flying up
in the film's rafters, where they sit
silent and blinking, just like the detectives
are doing now, down at the station,
hands on their sweaty half-windsors, necks
and heads half shadow in the light hung over
the only evidence, which is circumstantial:
a silver tie-clasp, the way he once stroked a cat.
It's going to be a long night.

Enough theories and guesses are thrown out
to build a forest—but it's a desolate one.

One where no one's listening to the thudding axe
as it fells slowly closer, where the small voice
humming, growing louder, isn't against fear of the dark,
or of being lost, it's just simply against,
against the whole thing in the first place:

—"I mean, no one even knew who he was."

I was to give a poetry reading at KGB and arrived early so as to get a drink in me. I know this speaks ill of me, but I don't remember whom I was reading with; just that I was reading first, he was reading second, and I was nervous enough that I kept reaching down to make sure my briefcase was still next to me. A minute before the reading, Star Black stood up and worked her way to the podium as I bent down to reach into my briefcase. My poems weren't there. The manila file folder I'd so carefully put them into an hour before was, I realized with a chill, still sitting on the bookshelf next to my apartment door. I told Star, who informed my fellow reader *he* was now reading first, and I gave someone I knew in the audience my apartment keys and twenty bucks for a cab. My friend made it back in about half an hour, just as the first reader was finishing up. Though the effects of my drink had worn off by then, and I didn't have time for another before I was due onstage, the rest of the evening was uneventful.

This wouldn't be so humiliating, except three days later I gave a separate reading, a prose reading, and despite the fact I'd been meticulous about having the right folder in my briefcase, it was only as I turned to the last page of my piece, as I was reading it up there at the podium, that I realized the last page was missing. My initial panic was so great I ran out of the room. Luckily, I remembered how the piece ended—it was about awkwardly dismounting a horse—and, after returning to the podium and having a brief discussion about the options with the audience, I acted the ending out. People later told me it was the best reading they'd seen in ages, that I should always forget my last page, though I didn't quite know how to take this.

LUCY GREALY

Rachel Hadas

Rachel Hadas is the author of twelve books of poetry, translations, and essays, including most recently *Halfway Down the Hall: New and Selected Poems* (Wesleyan University Press, 1998). The recipient of awards including a Guggenheim Fellowship in poetry, an Ingram Merrill Award, and an American Academy of Arts and Letters Award in literature, she teaches English at the Newark campus of Rutgers University. She has also taught writing at Princeton and Columbia Universities as well as at the Sewanee Writers Conference. A collection of her prose is forthcoming from the University of Michigan's Poets on Poetry series. She read at KGB on April 20, 1998.

IN THE GROVE

Forster says in *Aspects of the Novel*
that fictional characters come in flat and round.
Let us apply this binary division
also to the living and the dead.

It may come as a surprise to learn
the living are the flat ones.
You might expect the dead
to shrink to two dimensions,

but no, they thicken, put on bulk and plumpness
until they seem more solid than the skinny

shapes of the living as we scurry past
always on our way to someplace else.

I mourn my dead when I remember them.
The round slim trunks from flat as cut-outs grow
full enough to lean against, to touch,
to walk through. I can slip

in among them or I can stand still,
thinking, breathing, maybe weeping, till
they come to me (occasionally they will).
I conjure them and then when they surround me

I pause in their pale grove
though always on my way to someplace else.
As is well known, the living are en route.
To where? We do not ask. We know the answer.

Why is it so hard to understand?
The living are flat. The dead
are round but out of reach.
Cry out to them; they are seldom near

or even if they hear they do not answer.
Next get this through your head:
the dead are flat. They stand
impassively in rows like dominoes

until they lean and one by one they fall.
Therefore it follows, fool,
that it is the living who are round,
the living who take up far too much room,

jostle and crowd. At whom
am I angry if not at the living?
When I remember them, as I have said,
I mourn my dead—

the ripple family, the hallowed ghosts
dappled and camouflaged in greenish shade.
My dead . . . We never seem to say *my living.*
We say *my loved ones*

and our mortality seeps through the phrase.
Loved ones: those we plan to leave behind
when we join the dead in their rustling grove,
yellow to green. The trees are out of time,

not like the living, who keep whizzing past
from here to there, exhaustingly en route
to where if not
this slope of trees I enter with a thought?

Mary Stewart Hammond

Mary Stewart Hammond is the author of *Out of Canaan*, which was published by Norton and received the Great Lakes Colleges Association New Writers Award. Her poem "Hubris at White, Ga." won the *New England Review* and *Bread Loaf Quarterly*'s Narrative Poem Contest. Her work has appeared in *The Atlantic Monthly*, *The New Yorker*, and *The Paris Review*. She teaches advanced workshops in poetry at the Writers Voice at the West Side Y in New York City. She read at KGB on May 12, 1997.

THE GWB IN THE RAIN

Late winter. Ice cold and drained of color
as fingertips cut off from oxygen.
Heading south on the Henry Hudson

the road curves, and through the vertical
tangle of tree trunks and bare branches
the idea of a bridge appears, erased

and returned by the windshield wipers.
Suspenders thin as harp strings lift
the horizontal span to meet

a pair of silvery catenary curves
so much the color of the day
their outlines look drawn in pencil on the sky,

the volume of each cable, four feet
in diameter and made of enough
miles of wire to crank us halfway

to the moon, reading like paper
pouring through a watercolor,
like the silence in music. Water,

cliffs, sky, birds flicker in the Xs
and Vs of its bare piers and towers,
the latticed girders soaring up

through space singing with the economy
of a poem held captive by its form,
claiming no more of the heavens and earth

than necessary to do its job.
From outside the car, the landscape's palette
of greys and browns, and our black umbrella,

frame the steel bridge sliding off
into the clouds draped like angel hair
over the denuded trees filigreed on the Palisades.

To anyone standing on the New Jersey side
Manhattan would look the same, the bridge's
thrust vaporizing into the mists masking

the 179th Street anchorage, a picture
of just how real the connection
between Manhattan and America is.

To the figures on barges plying the river,
and on the brigantine materializing
under power from the white breath of the Hudson's

mouth, who see the bridge more nearly dead on,
the toy cars and trucks skimming its motion
east and west must seem to drive off the world.

As we watch, fog snuffs out the third dimension
and civilization (except for the baffled roar
of traffic), and the penciled bridge

fades, as if time had wound backward
to the blank page in Othmar Ammann's sketch pad,
leaving only the glimmer of a red lighthouse

for just such conditions, there
at the bottom left-hand edge of the waterscape,
close by the downstream flank of the bridge,

guarding Jeffrey's Point,
an artifact from our century's childhood,
freshly painted and well maintained as any

childhood, beckoning, not even ankle high
to the bridge, barely three humans high,
its bell silenced, its lens gone.

Bob Holman

Bob Holman's most recent CD is *In with the Out Crowd* (Mouth Almighty), and his latest book is *The Collect Call of the Wild* (Holt, 1995). He is editing a digital anthology, *The World of Poetry* (www.worldofpoetry.org), and is poetry guide at http://poetry.miningco.com. He teaches Exploding Text: Poetry Performance at Bard College. He read at KGB on April 14, 1997.

PERFORMANCE POEM

> *Voices. Voices. Listen, my heart, as only saints have listened;*
> *until the gigantic call lifted them off the ground; yet they kept*
> *on, impossibly, kneeling and didn't notice at all: so complete*
> *was their listening.*

> —RILKE

He's diving off the front of the stage!
You better bring the house lights up some,
The audience can't see him.
He's still screaming,
Screaming and dancing
And he's twirling the mic—
I dunno, should we turn off the mic?
I dunno, turn it up?
He's running around, he's twirling and
He's still like reading.
The book is in his hands, sort of, the people

Seem to like it, they're into it—
Maybe it's part of the act.

If it's part of the act he shoulda told us!
Now he's in the back of the house—he's
Still going strong. This is pretty
Amazing. I've never seen anything
Like this! He's running out
Of the theater—I can still hear him screaming
In the lobby. He's back in the house!
(What's he saying?—It's something about
It sounds like "lake snore freedom" . . .
I dunno. "Breaking down reason"?)
Oh shit! Oh shit oh shit—he's got a gun!

Christ! wait—awww, it's just one of those pop guns.
Shoots like firecrackers or popcorn or—
What about the hat? Still wearing the hat.
Holy—he's dying now, I mean he's acting like that,
Like he's dying. This is it for poetry in this house man,
I've had it.

He's just lying there.
The audience is wailing, they're keening
You know, like at a wake. No, I do not think
He's really dead. He's getting back up, see, I told
You—it's all part of the act!

It's all part of the end of the world.

What am I, the guy's father?

Come here! Look at the monitor yourself

He's ditched the mic somewhere,

Should I go get the mic?

Look! oh my God—he's, what's it called,

He's going up, he's levitating!

Holy shit! The roof, the roof is going up

Music is coming in

The crowd's up outta the chairs, man this is it

This is it I'm telling you—

Raising the fucking roof is what he's doing!

Now he's back on the stage with his poetry stuff

Yeah heh heh yeah,

He never left the stage

It's what his poem was about

I'm just saying what he's saying

Through the headset

Yeah, he's good

He's pretty good alright

But I could write something like that

Anybody could write something like that

Seems I've spent most of my adult life at poetry readings. I ran readings at St. Mark's Poetry Project for seven years, and slammed at the Nuyorican Poets Cafe for a similar cycle, but will never forget the very first reading I ever attended.

I'd just moved to New York City from New Richmond, Ohio, to become a poet, enrolling in Kenneth Koch's fantastic survey course at Columbia, a performance in itself. I noticed a few hand-drawn flyers around campus for a Poetry Reading, so I grabbed my notebook and headed over to Forlini's Third Phase, fully expecting to see all 150 of Prof. Koch's students, plus gobs of other poets-to-be.

The Third Phase was a brick room downstairs from a college pizza joint on 110th and Broadway, a kind of room I've grown very familiar with over the years. Dank, ill-lit, and primarily a corridor for the kitchen help, it was Mr. Forlini's desire to eke out the economic potential of this passageway, and, being unfit for anything, the words poetry reading came to mind. Actually, to ear, because it was Donald Lev, a totally great poet and one of the foremost poetry entrepreneurs of our time, who suggested to Mr. Forlini utilizing said basement as a site for verbal expression of ancient literary art, expecting to draw the vast hordes of poets attending Columbia, all hoping to follow the Beat path to Blakean ecstasy.

I was, of course, the only student who showed up, joining ten other humans who supported Lev's other readings. (If you need evidence on Lev's place in poetic history, I urge you to rent *Putney Swope* from your local videodrome: the poet who stops Putney and Fidel on a street corner is a Real Poet, in a role similar to Amiri Baraka's in *Bulworth*, Don Lev, doing his signature poem, "Hyn.")

A couple weeks later I saw an officially sanctioned reading at Columbia, two graduates from the class of '48, Allen Ginsberg and John Hollander. Ginsberg was already The Bard, and lashed into an unforgettable show; Hollander represented the tie-your-beard-to-the-podium and muffle-your-voice-in-the-book school perfectly.

In these two events are all the Ur- you need for the state of the art. Poetry still has a fierce crew of adherents who attend small readings in darkened basements (in fact, Don Lev still runs some). There continue to be Ginsbergian nightingales, glorious theatrical performers who fly words to ear and lift audience into orbits. And there are still poets who could care less about readings, thinking them strictly social excuses built round The Poem, which exists permanently inked in a book.

So here are the results, quick-cut, 1999: a book dedicated to a reading series in a bar, which, even while it's upstairs, still feels like somebody eking economics from a next-to-unusable space, a poetry kind of place. Don't forget that when Maxwell Bodenheim talked Max Gordon into starting the Village Vanguard, it was as a poetry bar, that when Michael Dorff first opened the Knitting Factory (tea the sole imbibement), it was poetry that was the first art in the house, and that it was the rAP mEETS pOETRY series that launched the Fez.

KGB's has, in its curators and comperes, the good sense and smarts to knock down the walls of the anthology wars which seem to divide poet from poet, unleashing a vitality that floods this volume like a good rendering. And KGB has the good luck to appear at a time when the infusion of energy from hip-hop, slam, and performance art has reinvigorated a sense of the performative in poetry.

At this gyration of the millennium, as poetry begins to take hold of new media—poetry videos, CDs, films, Web sites—the simple reading of a poem aloud still holds the center as the most complex and invigorating mode of transmission for the art. It's the audience that writes the poem, each to his own, each taking the wild ride of language connecting us one to the other, to our diverse histories. I used to say, A poem's not written till it's read. These days it might be, A poem doesn't happen till it's heard. And, it might be added, A poem's not over till it's been heckled.

BOB HOLMAN

Virginia Hooper

Virginia Hazel Hooper, born in 1955, received her undergraduate degree from Harvard University, where she studied art history, and her M.F.A. from Columbia University, where she was a Merit Fellow in the writing division. Her poetry has appeared in many anthologies and journals, *The Best American Poetry, Primary Trouble: An Anthology of Contemporary Poetry, American Poetry Review, Postmodern Culture,* and *Pequod* among them. She is coauthor of several books in the Art History Through Touch and Sound series and contributes fiction to *Penthouse.* In addition to teaching at the Museum of Modern Art in New York, she has written museum audioguides and visual arts commentary. For many years she was an editor for *American Letters and Commentary.* She lives in New York City, where she writes on medical issues and is working on a novel. She read at KGB on May 5, 1997.

A READING

You are impatient, says the oracle.
The weather has arrived cloudy, another day's conclusion
Shot with unravelling paths set back

From the shore. An ocean breeze reshuffles the cards
Across the deck, disorder restored to pattern,
A chance you pattern yourself toward.

Prompted to rethink your question,
Which might, with grace, lift you above the determined
Arrangement currents have washed you against,

You play another hand. A chance you pattern yourself
Against lifts back through selves
You have assumed, fools sprung from oracle

Beginnings framed inside the gold-leaf border
Of the cards played in patience
When it wasn't in the cards to share the evening

With another. And what of crossed destiny?
Teased out of solitaire, prompted by impatience,
You think you have been courted by the cards.

Strange, how this pattern unravels
Inside the tale arranged for the oracle's pleasure.
A link, afterall, you think.

Richard Howard

Richard Howard was born in Cleveland, Ohio, in 1929. He was educated at Columbia University and the Sorbonne. He has translated over 150 works from the French. The most recent of his eleven books of poems is *Trappings* (Counterpoint); for his third, *Untitled Subjects*, he was awarded the Pulitzer Prize in 1970. He is a member of the American Academy of Arts and Letters and a chancellor of the Academy of American Poets. In 1996 he was named a fellow of the MacArthur Foundation. He is poetry editor for *The Paris Review* and *Western Humanities Review* and teaches at Columbia University. He read at KGB on April 21, 1997.

MRS. EDEN IN TOWN FOR THE DAY

Sorry I'm late. I had to drive *way* out of my
    way to pick up coyote piss—
for the garden. We use about a quart a month:
    it really does deter the deer.

This man I know at the zoo keeps it for me, for
    a group of us, actually:
all gardeners. He happens to *be* a keeper—
    of coyotes, hyenas, wolves,

whatever—and he keeps coyote piss as well
    (under refrigeration, of course),

sells it right there at the zoo. I hate the long drive,
    but I love having no more deer

in the garden. Expensive, too, or should I say
    dear, but it's definitely not
a competitive item — where else can you get
    coyote piss that's full strength,

not reconstituted from crystals or some kind
    of concentrate? It has to be
fresh — from the wild — or the damn deer just ignore it.
    I wonder how such merchandise

would be collected? Tom says there's something
    they call a Texas Catheter,
really not much more than a perforated
    condom attached to a bottle . . .

Have you ever seen such goings-on at a *zoo*?
    Well neither have I — but of course
I wasn't looking . . . Who would be, unless you *knew* . . .
    However he gets hold of it,

it works! Today our keeper told me *human hair*
    has the same effect, on most deer —
we could try that. Think how much cheaper, for one thing:
    a year's sweepings from Tom's barber

would cost less than a week's gasoline! Even so,
    people's hair . . . Better the other:
I wonder which animals would keep off if we tried
    our own instead of coyote's?

moose   *dik-dik*   *gazelle*   *caribou*   *hartebeest*   *gnu*

Richard Howard, pinch-hitting for his ailing friend John Hollander, read poems from the time the two "were writing poems against each other." The poets Peter Nickowitz (left), Vincent Katz (second from left), and Julia Kasdorf are among those in rapt attention.

95

Marie Howe

Marie Howe was born in 1950. Her first book, *The Good Thief*, was selected by Margaret Atwood for the National Poetry Series. Her most recent collection of poems is *What the Living Do* (Norton, 1997). She teaches at Sarah Lawrence College and has received a fellowship from the National Endowment for the Arts. She read at KGB on April 13, 1997.

SIXTH GRADE

The afternoon the neighborhood boys tied me and Mary Lou Mahar
to Donny Ralph's father's garage doors, spread-eagled,
it was the summer they chased us almost every day.

Careening across the lawns they'd mowed for money,
on bikes they threw down, they'd catch us, lie on top of us,
then get up and walk away.

That afternoon Donny's mother wasn't home.
His nine sisters and brothers gone—even Gramps, who lived with them,
gone somewhere—the backyard empty, the big house quiet.

A gang of boys. They pulled the heavy garage doors down,
and tied us to them with clothesline,
and Donny got the deer's leg severed from the buck his dad had killed

the year before, dried up and still fur-covered, and sort of
poked it at us, dancing around the blacktop in his sneakers, laughing.
Then somebody took it from Donny and did it.

And then somebody else, and somebody after him.
Then Donny pulled up Mary Lou's dress and held it up,
and she began to cry, and I became a boy again, and shouted Stop,

and they wouldn't.
Then a girl-boy, calling out to Charlie, my best friend's brother,
who wouldn't look

Charlie! to my brother's friend who knew me
Stop them. And he wouldn't.
And then more softly, and looking directly at him, I said, Charlie.

And he said Stop. And they said What? And he said Stop it.
And they did, quickly untying the ropes, weirdly quiet,
Mary Lou still weeping. And Charlie? Already gone.

I'd never been to KGB until the night I read there with Charlie Smith. My
sister and her two daughters were visiting me that week from our home-
town, Rochester, N.Y. Emma and Hayley were at that time eleven and
eight, had never been to New York, had never seen taxicabs, homeless
people, or so many people walking down the street at one time. When we
walked into the club, it was crowded and dark and smoky—everything
seemed red, the curtains, the tablecloths, the light itself. The girls took,
with my sister, the only seats available, at the bar, where Melvin Bukiet
poured them free Cokes, which they sipped through straws.

The room only seemed to get smokier as I began to speak. And I don't know how to explain it really, but it was transporting to see, through the haze and the clumps of people crowded together dressed in black, the faces of these two girls whom I loved—their cheeks flushed, their gaze clear and steady, leaning from their barstools a little back against the bar, listening to me.

I read the poems from my book, aware that I was reading to them—for the first time—to Emma and Hayley. And what can I tell you? It's not that I wished the poems were different from what they were. It's that I saw the faces of these two girls through that crowd and I wished I had something to say to them, or to ask them—something that would speak to their exquisite girlness, their newness and their beauty, or something that would speak of it—something that would praise it, something that would raise it up then and now for all to see.

We finished the reading, the girls put on their coats—I think we went somewhere for hot chocolate, then back out into the city, into our mutual adventure. But I can't help but wonder—what if we wrote our poems to the whole tribe? To the very old people among us, and to the eleven-year-old girls, and to the eighteen-year-old boys, to the sixty-two-year-old women and men—perhaps we do—although I realized that night that I didn't. What if I wrote directly to those two faces looking so clearly back at me? What would I say to them? What would I ask? What poetry?

MARIE HOWE

Lawrence Joseph

Lawrence Joseph was born in Detroit in 1948 and educated at the University of Michigan, Cambridge University, and the University of Michigan Law School. His books of poems include *Shouting at No One* (1983), which received the Starrett Poetry Prize, and *Curriculum Vitae* (1988), both published in the Pitt Poetry Series. His most recent book is *Before Our Eyes* (Farrar, Straus and Giroux, 1993). He has received a poetry fellowship from the National Endowment for the Arts and is a professor of law at St. John's University. He lives with his wife, the painter Nancy Van Goethem, in New York City. He read at KGB on October 27, 1997.

WHEN ONE IS FEELING ONE'S WAY

I

The sky was red and the earth got hot,
hot, like a hundred degrees, I mean.
"Stay cool," the monk was said to have said,
"you've got a long way yet to go." A monk,
say, of Hué, who, to protest the killing
of innocents, is dragging an altar onto
—yes it was, downtown, Woodward Avenue.
So what else is new? One new
voice mail message. A woman, a certain woman,
recently has been seen
rubbing both eyes with the palms of her hands.

II

Two things, two things that are
interesting, are history and grammar.
Down in among the foundations of
the intelligence the chemistries
of words. "Those fault lines of risk
buried deep in the global financial
landscape . . ." What of it? Nothing but
the same resistance since
the time of the Gracchi, that against
private interests' arrogation
of the common wealth—against
the turgid, precious language of pseudo-erudition,
false-voiced God-talkers and power freaks,
thugs, that's what they are, with no idea
what it is they're bringing down.

III

A pause. Any evening, every evening.
When one is feeling one's way,
the pattern is small and complex.
At center, a moral issue, but composed,
and first. Looks to me like,
across the train yards a blurred sun
setting behind the high ground
on the other side of the Hudson,
overhead purple and pink.

A changing set of marginal options.
Whole lots of amplified light.

IV

Oh, I get the idea. That image,
the focal point of a concave mirror,
is old.

And that which is unintermitted
and fragile, wild and fragile (there,
behind the freighter's yellow puffs
of smoke; God, no, I haven't
forgotten it) is, I said, still
fragile, still proud.

A poetry reading, or poetry readings, that I remember most . . .
Two, in particular, come to mind.
One, the late eighties, the Morgan Library, James Merrill reading and discussing the poems of C. P. Cavafy. Merrill, who spoke modern Greek, read several of Cavafy's poems (I don't remember which ones) in the original. He talked about how Cavafy would, in Greek, alter meter to fit the sounds and syntax of colloquial speech, that everything Cavafy did formally (his use of rhyme and off-rhyme, when he used it, for example) adhered to the sounds and syntax of common, vulgate speech. He also read from E. M. Forster's essay "The Poetry of C. P. Cavafy" (which is found in Forster's book *Pharos and Pharillon*):

> Yes, it is Mr. Cavafy, and he is going either from his flat to the office, or
> from his office to the flat. If the former, he vanishes when seen, with a
> slight gesture of despair. If the latter, he may be prevailed upon to begin
> a sentence—an immense complicated yet shapely sentence, full of

parentheses that never get mixed and of reservations that really do reserve; a sentence that moves with logic to its foreseen end, yet to an end that is always more vivid and thrilling than one foresaw. It deals with the tricky behaviour of the Emperor Alexius Comnenus in 1096, or with olives, their possibilities and price, or with the fortunes of friends, or George Eliot, or the dialects of the interior of Asia Minor. It is delivered with equal ease in Greek, English, or French. And despite its intellectual richness and human outlook, despite the matured clarity of its judgments one feels that it too stands at a slight angle to the universe.

Merrill looked up from the podium. "Both the sentence of the poet," he said, "and the poet, too, both"—he smiled—"both stand at a slight angle to the universe."

The other reading that stays in my mind was in Ann Arbor, in February 1970, at Canterbury House, at the time an Episcopal Church and meeting place for those who believed in and practiced principles of nonviolence. It was a cold, clear, moonlit evening; the reading began late, around ten o'clock. Robert Bly read translations of poems by Pablo Neruda, César Vallejo, and Miguel Hernández. People were standing, sitting in the aisles— people you usually didn't see at poetry readings. The mood was half-earnest and, you might say, half-inflamed with rage against war and murder:

> The human soul was threshed out like maize in the endless granary of
> defeated actions, of mean things that happened

—the first two lines of Neruda's "The Heights of Machu Picchu, III," a poem I may have heard that evening (James Wright's translation);

> Moon: it is no use flying anyway,
> so you go up in a flame of scattered opals;
> maybe you are my heart, who is like a gypsy,
> who loafs in the sky, shedding poems like tears!

—the final stanza of Vallejo's "A Divine Falling of Leaves," another poem I may have heard that evening (again in James Wright's translation).

I almost forgot. There was Adrienne Rich's reading at DIA, in '95 or '96. The voice, the depth and the intensity; what is remembered, what lasts, is the concentration, the intensity, the truth, of the voice. And—how could I forget?—James Schuyler's reading at DIA. Sixty-five years old, his first reading ever, when DIA was still downtown. Nineteen eighty-eight. November. An hour before the reading, a line formed in the street, hundreds, in the cold, up around the corner. Schuyler sat as he read, under spotlights used for the video camera, making no comments about the poems, often, slowly, taking a sip of water. With uncharacteristic immodesty and characteristic accuracy, Schuyler wrote Anne Dunn, afterwards, that he was "a fucking sensation." Everyone who was there (and the number seems to increase as the years go by) will tell you that he or she has never been to another poetry reading—

Then things got better, greater:
Mildred Bailey sang immortal hits
indelibly
permanently
marked by that voice
with built-in laughter
perfect attack

—likc that.

LAWRENCE JOSEPH

Lawrence Joseph basked in the critical and popular success of his nonfiction book Lawyerland.

Vickie Karp

Vickie Karp was born in New York City in 1953. In 1988 her documentary film, *Marianne Moore: In Her Own Image*, ran as part of the Voices and Visions series on PBS. Her poems have been chosen twice for inclusion in *The Best American Poetry*. She has received poetry fellowships from the National Endowment for the Arts and from the New York Foundation for the Arts. Her book of poems, *A Taxi to the Flames*, was published by the University of South Carolina Press in 1999. She read at KGB on February 17, 1997.

HARM

First, you took the parakeet out of its cage,
Its body warm and folded, a blue-green kite
With a surprised heart. Then, you scoured the metal,
The door a loose pocket of bars on two wire hinges,
The tray floor, the seed and water dishes,
The clawed perches, the swing and its endless dialogue
With the invisible. Slowly, you removed the racks
From the dishwasher and placed the cage in it.
We laughed at your ingenuity, at the way
It expressed your secret ambition to be
The cleverest, the funniest,
The one least mauled by the predictable.
And I think I knew then that I would carry on this hope
Of yours. There is such harm in love.

But let it be the green and blue acrobat it is,
A tropical danger in the midst of my body,
The body that you built for me.
Let it be the cage you cared for from which
Birdsong was pulled into the cool and colorless air.

Years ago I did a reading at Chumley's, the Greenwich Village tavern, and they pounded the veal scallopini in exact cadence to my description of a lovesick beating heart.

VICKIE KARP

(Left to right) John Scherzer, Erin Colligan, and Kathleen E. Krause, students in the graduate writing program at New School University, fulfilled degree requirements at KGB.

Karl Kirchwey

Born in Boston in 1956 and educated at Yale College and Columbia University, Karl Kirchwey is the author of three collections of poetry, *A Wandering Island* (1990; recipient of the Poetry Society of America's Norma Farber First Book Award), *Those I Guard* (1993), and *The Engrafted Word* (1998). He has served as director of the Unterberg Poetry Center of the Ninety-second Street Y since 1987. He was awarded the 1994 Rome Prize in literature and has also received grants from the National Endowment for the Arts and from the Ingram Merrill and John Simon Guggenheim Memorial Foundations. He lives in Manhattan with his wife and two children. He read at KGB on June 2, 1997.

ORACULAR DEGENERATION

Why, he aimed the car right at that girl!
 —in your dreams: a Taurus for Europa's acceleration.
He aimed a cur right at that griddle!
 —Excuse me, sir: we are not dogeaters.
He aimed the curl right at that gar!
 —absorbed soundlessly into the flank of the wave.
He aimed a Kurd right at that Gaul!
 —at the School of International and Public Affairs.
He aimed the churl right at that Grendel!
 —or dying in a slow spiral, not from hunger.
He aimed the krill right at that Kir Royal!
 —a blush drink fit for a sulfurbottom.

He aimed a corpse right at that gallimander!

—what transports pink granite transports flesh.

'e aimed a whinger, Cor, roight a' that gel!

—but the eye of God still lights the world.

He omm'ed a curtsy right at the spiritual!

—but the Man Upstairs wasn't listening.

He aimed a Coors right at heaven's zone and girdle

—but she sidestepped the can without difficulty.

In my fifteen seasons at the Ninety-second Street Y's Unterberg Poetry Center, I have attended more than five hundred literary readings by more than a thousand writers. This is quite a canvas, and it contains some bright spots and some rather dark ones. The best moments have had one thing in common: the primal connection between a poet and his or her audience, a group of listeners bound by the spoken word. And it has been my experience that this connection cannot be duplicated by any of the "virtual" media; in fact, it cannot be duplicated by reading a poem silently on the printed page, either. This power of poetry, when read well aloud, to explain itself is part of what makes poetry readings such an important cultural phenomenon.

A poet who never shows up for an onstage interview, leaving a restless crowd of hundreds, which another poet (friend of the first) must calm by singing and reciting his work to them; a poet who goes onstage drunk and reads for an hour and a half, martyring a younger poet whose reading is to follow his own, as the crowd trickles away; a poet whose love of English is great, but not greater than the accent of his native language, so that he eschews a translator and leaves the audience clueless through much of his reading; a poet who explains too much; a poet who explains too little; a poet who makes himself into an onstage buffoon as a willful gesture against the urbanities of New York; a poet whose work, long anticipated by the audience, is counterpointed perfectly by the rural drawl of his prose interludes and who, with a dramatic flourish worthy of Leporello in the catalog aria in *Don Giovanni,* pulls out of his pocket onstage an accordioning

adding machine tape on which a new poem is written; a poet's last read-
ing, from the prose memoir of his own life, his voice roughened by laryngi-
tis; a Scots poet, reading his savage version of the flaying of Marsyas from
Ovid; an English poet, reading his own wildly cinematic accounts of the
ancient slaughter on the plains outside Troy; the unexpected humor of an
ascetic lyric poet's accounts of the collapse of a marriage; a poet reading
jazz-inflected work with the pianist Tommy Flanagan accompanying him; a
North Carolina fiction writer's performance of "When Malindy Sings" in per-
fect dialect; Roscoe Lee Browne's soliloquy of forgiveness in the person of
the Greek hero Philoctetes, as translated by a contemporary Irish poet; the
last great Yiddish poet, an old man come to New York from Israel: well,
these are a few of the readings I will always remember.

And the bright places in the canvas are more numerous than the
dark ones.

KARL KIRCHWEY

Wayne Koestenbaum

Wayne Koestenbaum is the author of three books of poetry: *Ode to Anna Moffo and Other Poems* (1990), *Rhapsodies of a Repeat Offender* (1994), and *The Milk of Inquiry* (1999). As critic he has written *Double Talk: The Erotics of Male Literary Collaboration* (1989), *The Queen's Throat: Opera, Homosexuality, and the Mystery of Desire* (1993; nominated for a National Book Critics Circle Award), and *Jackie Under My Skin: Interpreting an Icon* (1995). He wrote the libretto for the opera *Jackie O* and received a Whiting Writers' Award in 1994. He is a professor of English in the Ph.D. program of the City University of New York. He read at KGB on October 20, 1997.

GAUDY SLAVE TRADER

Everyone hates the gaudy slave trader, with good reason.
He represents the worst of humankind.

However, in certain moods I appreciate his gaudiness —
I'm prone to it myself
Tonight I feel it return.
Can you advise? How might I purge myself
before it arrives? I remember a restaurant

with gaudy decor and exceptional seafood appetizers
in San Francisco. The restaurant will close,
or has already closed, but I stand here as witness
that it once existed.

I am not a slave trader but I am gaudy
is the only conclusion I can draw.

Even the act of drawing a conclusion
resembles weeping, the rheumy look my mother said she remembered,
and I didn't ask her when she first noticed it,

though she might have told me, had I persevered.
I never persevere. That is my first problem.

I should tabulate the problems,
but I resist tabulation.

One winter afternoon may be cold enough to change my mind,
but until then, resistance will be my only form of slumber.

The first poetry reading I ever gave, a group endeavor, in 1986, took place in a church—desanctified? Its reconfigured interior reminded me of El Morocco. Many friends loyally showed up, and they laughed at lines I hadn't recognized were funny. Suddenly I imagined moonlighting as a cabaret raconteur, a stand-up comic.

That first reading was my swan song as Lenny Bruce. And yet I still remember the surprising laughter, and the dream of developing a nightclub act.

WAYNE KOESTENBAUM

Yusef Komunyakaa

Yusef Komunyakaa was born in Bogalusa, Louisiana, in 1947. His most recent books of poetry, both published by Wesleyan University Press, are *Neon Vernacular* (1993), which was awarded the Kingsley Tufts Award and the 1994 Pulitzer Prize, and *Thieves of Paradise* (1998). In 1997 he received the Hanes Poetry Prize. He has taught at Indiana University and at Washington University in St. Louis, and is now a professor of creative writing at Princeton University. He has a volume forthcoming in the University of Michigan Press's Poets on Poetry series. He read at KGB on March 30, 1998.

CHASTITY BELT

Invisible catches & secret hooks, bone
Within bone & trick locks.
If a man needs this to hold
Love in place, the master of keys

Will always bite his nails
To the quick. Tooled leather,
Laced mail & jeweled bronze.
Before his departure over a body

Of tremulant water, he turns
The key in the lock as they kiss.
Like something alive, it sways
Beneath his armor from a gold chain

Around his neck, to the rhythm
Of galloping hooves. Two days
Later, with a dagger in his belly,
Thick fingers tear the key from his throat.

Yusef Komunyakaa, surrounded by autograph seekers, read some of his jazz poems at KGB. In "Twilight Seduction" Komunyakaa explores his affinity for Duke Ellington, with whom he shares a birthday (April 29). Duke would have been ninety-nine when Yusef read for us in 1998.

Wendy Wilder Larsen

Wendy Wilder Larsen was born in Boston, moved to California when she was five, and has been traveling ever since. Nineteen seventy brought her to Vietnam, where she taught Vietnamese teachers Shakespeare and Romantic poetry. *Shallow Graves*, her book of narrative verse about that year and Tran Thi Nga, the Vietnamese woman she met there, was the first book about the war in Vietnam from an American and a Vietnamese woman's point of view. She lives in Manhattan and is a member of the International Council of the Museum of Modern Art. She is on the board of Poets House. A passionate bird-watcher, she found inspiration for this poem on an early spring walk in Central Park. She read at KGB on May 11, 1998.

BLUEBIRD IN CUTLEAF BEECH

there is no pigment in blue feathers
all other colors are scattered out
blue is what's left

that particular shade of delphinium petals
falling on my mother's white lacquer table
under the rotunda in summer

the color of distance
the pain in my father's watery blues
in that picture in the navy

blue
the faded pinafore in my portrait
hands folded, same pale eyes

the color we love to contemplate
not because it comes to us
but because it draws us after it

the will-o'-the-wisp's bluish glow
that loses us at the crossroads
lures us into swamps

blue then
this absence
this scattering

still I would search
and call out

there

mother
father

bluebird

I went to a boarding school in Middleburg, Virginia, called Foxcroft. We wore uniforms and marched with guns ("pieces" not "guns," we were taught to say), but we also had wonderful teachers. I remember my first poetry reading sophomore year. A marvelous woman, called Isabella Stewart Gardner, stood on the stage, her red hair a halo above the podium, and in a deep voice with a Boston accent delivered lines I will never forget: "West of now and far from Illinois our laughter tinkled among the teacups." The scansion is mine as I have never seen the poem, but I decided then and there that I would be a poet.

WENDY WILDER LARSEN

Wendy Wilder Larsen's Vietnam poems continue to move audiences. In "Orphanage" the poet brings candy and magazines and toys for the orphans but not enough to go around, with the result that the children "popped the balloons/choked on the candies/[and] shredded the magazines." The incident becomes a metaphor for the unintended consequences of U.S. foreign aid.

Ann Lauterbach

Ann Lauterbach was born and grew up in Manhattan. Among her thirteen books, which include collaborations with artists and five poetry collections, are *Clamor* (1991), *And for Example* (1994), and *On a Stair* (1997), all from Viking Penguin. She has received fellowships from the Guggenheim and MacArthur Foundations and has taught in several graduate writing programs, most recently at City College and Bard College. She read at KGB on October 27, 1997.

THE NOVELIST SPEAKS
for Don DeLillo

Dependency on *and*
and finally this word, this simple monosyllabic word,
more important than Paris.
           —the American language
             —from the American

street games, baseball, adspeak,
films, riffs,
Italian-American slang of the lost Bronx
the first fiction
        to repeat the experience

           no coincidence
           an enormous pleasure in remembering
pleasure
the unmentionable shame
the last thing

a culture of endless complaint
of pleasure whose existence we suppress
this element of pleasure
the language
in curious opposition to the enormous

                  of war

                  and fate
        a dream release that history needs to escape

                  brutal confinements
      self-preservation

against the vast and uniform death
to fashion its most
enduring work
      to wonder in those cold war years

        terribly sundered
          what it all meant

iconic fury   the atomic bomb itself

our lives
a fiction
unreal to ourselves
outside our comprehension

lists are a form of cultural hysteria

three great attractions

informed

and jazz

All language taken from a talk given by Don DeLillo

During her KGB reading Ann Lauterbach (left) commented on her penchant for "unfinished" works and wondered whether she was alone in this predilection. Came a small voice from the crowd: "Schubert." Eugene Richie (right) read at KGB with Pace University colleague Charles North.

Lucie Brock-Broido, who read with Liam Rector at KGB in February 1999, runs the graduate poetry writing program at Columbia University's School of the Arts.

Harry Mathews (center) read us Wordsworth's "I Wandered Lonely as a Cloud" transformed by a system of word substitutions. For example, the word imbeciles replaces daffodils. ("And then my heat with plenty fills/And dances with the imbeciles.")

*Codirector David Lehman shares a laugh with bar owner Denis Woychuk
(left) and poet Jason Shinder (center). David read from his latest book,
The Daily Mirror, a collection of poems written one-a-day over the course
of a year.*

David Lehman

David Lehman was born in New York City in 1948. He is the author of four poetry books, including *The Daily Mirror* (Scribner), a selection of the poems he has written since he began writing a poem a day as an experiment. *The Last Avant-Garde: The Making of the New York School of Poets* is his latest work of nonfiction (Doubleday Anchor, 1999). He is on the core faculty of the graduate writing programs at Bennington College and New School University. He also teaches a "great poems" course at New York University. He is the series editor of *The Best American Poetry*, which he initiated in 1988, and is codirector of the Monday night poetry series at KGB. He read at KGB on April 27, 1998.

THE PROPHET'S LANTERN

What's new?
The question implies a possibility:
that the old saw wasn't true,
the one that says there's nothing
new under the sun.
The prophet rests in the shade.

Not black but a dark shade
of blue is the shade in which the new
growth, protected from the sun,
tests the possibility
that the prophet's vision of nothing
could not come true.

The prophet knows true
north is the direction of a shade
after death when nothing
further can be done, no new
remedy can revive the possibility
of new light from an ancient sun.

In the glare of the midday sun
things that were true
at night grow faint. The possibility
of love's warmth in a cool shade
is what's needed: something new,
not just a reiteration of nothing.

"The sun shone on the nothing
new," he wrote. Blank was the sun,
the masses quit the church, and new
pigeons ate stale bread. The true
isn't equal to the good; there's a shade
of difference between the possibility

that judgment is futile and the possibility
that it can't be evaded, as nothing
in our destiny can be. Linger in the shade,
we may as well. We cannot bear too much sun
if the one thing that is true
is that everything is possible, nothing new.

Yet news travels fast. Nothing lasts.
The possibility of love among the shades
remains as true as when the sun was new.

The most astonishing thing I ever heard at a poetry reading? It was in 1971 or '72. I had gone to Cambridge University on a Kellett Fellowship. Robert Lowell, then the American poet best known and most admired in Britain, came to Cambridge to read. I wrote about what happened in my poem "Cambridge, 1972":

> Professor H., introducing Robert Lowell
> At a poetry reading, called him "one of the greatest living poets"
> Adding: "And I think we can safely remove the word living from that
>   description."
> He meant it as a compliment, but Lowell looked ashen-faced.

I read that poem at KGB the night Lawrence Joseph—my old Cambridge pal, who figures in the poem—read for us in October 1997.

DAVID LEHMAN

Rika Lesser

Rika Lesser was educated at Yale and Columbia Universities and is the author of three books of poems: *Growing Back: Poems 1972–1992* (University of South Carolina Press, 1997), *All We Need of Hell* (University of North Texas Press, 1995), and *Etruscan Things* (Braziller, 1983). She has received many honors for her translations, including the Landon Translation Prize of the Academy of American Poets, the Poetry Translation Prize of the Swedish Academy, and a Fulbright-Hays Research Grant for Sweden in spring 1999. Her other awards include the Amy Lowell Poetry Travelling Fellowship and an Ingram Merrill Foundation Award. She has taught at Columbia, Yale, George Washington University, and the Poetry Center of the Ninety-second Street Y. She read at KGB on November 17, 1997.

TRANSLATION

Lost: the Original, its Reason and its Rhyme,
Words whose meanings do not change through time,
"The soul in paraphrase," the heart in prose,
Strictures or structures, meter, *les mots justes;*
"The owlet umlaut" when the text was German,
Two hours of sleep each night, hapax legomenon,
A sense of self, fidelity, one's honor,
Authorized versions from a living donor.

Found in translation: someone else's voice:
Ringing and lucid, whispered, distant, true

That in its rising accents falls to you,

Wahlverwandtschaft, a fortunate choice,

A call to answer, momentary grace,

Unbidden, yours; a way to offer praise.

Attending one poetry reading really did "change my life." It was at the Guggenheim Museum in September 1982, part of a Scandinavia Today program. Arranged by the Academy of American Poets and the American-Scandinavian Foundation, it was a panel of several Scandinavian poets and translators; I found myself wedged between Finnish and Norwegian guests. A translator of dead poets back then (Rilke, Ekelöf), I didn't at that time know the work of the Swedish poet Göran Sonnevi very well because I didn't much like what I had read. What was so captivating about his four-hundred page poem, "The Impossible," which trickled down page after page, hugging the left margin? His texts seemed tracts on linguistics, mathematics, politics, subjects about which I preferred to read in other forms. But later I heard Sonnevi read—alphabetically last, by which time I was pacing in the glass booth above the auditorium—*read* is not the right word, neither is *intone* or *incant;* the word *intonation* took on an entirely new meaning as I listened. At the end of each enjambed and often brief line the voice rose; the stress on each word was extraordinary, the stress on the first word of a new line even more extraordinary. As the underlying rhythmic patterns shifted, the poet's body subtly but perceptibly moved with them. There were pauses of different durations, beautiful silences. The sensation of hearing that voice for the first time was sensual, nearly erotic. Like a knife . . . through water. . . . I have been translating his poetry, his unending poem that continues from book to book, not quite continuously ever since.

RIKA LESSER

Rika Lesser (right) read her poems and translations to the delight of old friend Charles Naylor.

Harvard contemporaries Donald Hall (left) and John Ashbery reminisce about college days. In the background, Pittsburgh Tribune *reviewer Dennis Loy Johnson sweet-talks main squeeze Valerie Merians. Stacey Harwood, smiling, and camera-shy Michael Malinowitz, who read at KGB in March 1999, complete the picture.*

Thomas Lux

Thomas Lux was born in Massachusetts in 1946. He teaches at Sarah Lawrence College and has received fellowships from the Guggenheim Foundation and the National Endowment for the Arts. His most recent books are *Selected Poems: 1975–1995* (Houghton Mifflin, 1997) and *The Blind Swimmer: Selected Early Poems, 1970–1975* (Adastra, 1996). He read at KGB on December 1, 1997.

PLAGUE VICTIMS CATAPULTED OVER WALLS INTO BESIEGED CITY

Early germ
warfare. The dead
hurled this way turn like wheels
in the sky. Look: there goes
Larry the Shoemaker, barefoot, over the wall,
and Mary Sausage Stuffer, see how she flies,
and the Hatter twins, both at once, soar
over the parapet, little Tommy's elbow bent
as if in a salute,
and his sister, Mathilde, she follows him,
arms outstretched, through the air,
just as she did
on earth.

I and two other poets arrived at a well-known progressive college for a scheduled reading. It was the spring, I believe, of 1973. It was pouring rain. We entered the small amphitheater (big enough to hold a few hundred people) to find there was one person in the audience. And he was unconscious from a drug overdose. We called an ambulance for him. He was sitting up and smiling when it arrived. In the meantime no one else had shown up for the reading. We stood around looking at each other for a while and then walked back out into the rain.

THOMAS LUX

With many Sarah Lawrence College students in attendance, Tom Lux read "The Voice You Hear When You Read Silently": "It is your voice/saying, for example, the word barn . . ./and a sensory constellation/is lit: horse-gnawed stalls,/hayloft, black heat tape wrapping/a water pipe."

Elizabeth Macklin

Elizabeth Macklin is the author of *A Woman Kneeling in the Big City* (Norton, 1992) and was awarded the Amy Lowell Poetry Travelling Scholarship for 1998–99. Her poems have appeared in *The Paris Review*, the *Boston Review*, *The New Yorker*, and elsewhere. She won the "poetry coaster" contest sponsored by Brooklyn Brewery in 1997. "The House Style" first appeared in *Open City*. She read at KGB on May 19, 1997.

THE HOUSE STYLE

was only an etiquette, a habit of speech not spoken
but imprinted: half grammar, half manner—salutation
and closing, as if at the end of an evening
a guest at the door were indeed provisioned
for the nightlong siege of information.

Burn marks, say, beside serial commas' courtesy:
1, 2, and 3—for one at a time was shock enough
to register. It was an etiquette invented over time
for a time of disaster, a breath of air
between sorrows. A collection of colliding customs:

a looseleaf of spellings in common— "focussed,"
"vermillion," "coöperation"—with evolving nouns
of place or feeling. Intent could be seen,

so sorrow could be detected, a column of smoke
above a campfire in Genesis, where the law was

only a bivouac. Everything hinged on intentionality:
intentionality governed every step toward a stop
or other outcome. And, just as the editor
in pencil requested "a quiet proof," and down the hall
the faintest of longhands copied the questions clearly

ready for answers ("Is this intentional? . . . Want this?
. . . This what you intended?") the style itself
was proof—a set of protocols—from when generals themselves
admitted to a need for sustenance, peace, the wartime elixir-
medication. It was assumed there would be an intention.

And so content the attending grammarians attended to style:
the crowd of diaereses, marks of punctuation and emphasis;
details scouting behaviors and landscapes; volition in idiom,
headlines in small capitals—a civil war of distinctions observed
elided. Not a phrenology, though—in truth—almost a religion.

I was not at this reading, but was told of it—passionately and in detail—by
a woman who was, when she handed me a tape. I wrote this for an essay
about something else (not readings); the taped evening is more strongly in
my mind than anything I've been to, except maybe memorials (Howard
Moss's, Amy Clampitt's, John Berryman's):

On December 8, 1986, at the Ninety-second Street Y, for the cente-
nary of Emily Dickinson's death, the actress Linda Hunt read an evening of
sixty-odd poems—many of which she'd learned by heart, having typed out
a manuscript for herself, a script, assimilating Dickinson, whom she hadn't

really read before. Reading aloud, Hunt entirely excised the silliness we can sometimes hear in Dickinson's rhythm and rhyme; she slowed the poems down to the pace of human speech (of a quick-witted, stylized-Amherst-parlor kind), and spoke the full range of the intonations in them— "internal difference, where the Meanings, are," which in her reading became the turning point of "There's a certain slant of light," even the point of it—as well as displaying an entirely unsilly humor. By showing to what extent so many of Dickinson's deceptively conclusive last lines were actually inconclusive, concludable only in the large, "internal" silences that follow them, Hunt drew attention back to the true shocks: the startling weight of reverie, in one of the briefest examples, the near-epigram

> To make a prairie it takes a clover and one bee,
> One clover, and a bee,
> And revery.
> The revery alone will do,
> If bees are few.

In Hunt's reading, we were in a smallish 1890s New England room, not so many years after hearing of the prairie for the first time, with all its new, Pascalian empty space and solitude. The comedic charge of "one bee," was so overturned (and so amplified) by "revery," by all the audible space around it, the thought became dizzying. And the last two lines, which at first had seemed mere recovery room—a light, half-dismissive reminder for the shaken ("revery alone")—in the subsequent silence ("revery alone") took on their more acute meaning: such empty space, "bees are few."

ELIZABETH MACKLIN

James Tate and Dara Wier kicked off the spring 1999 season at KGB.
Both read knockout new works. Wier's "Tyranny of Affection" begins:
"One television brings a family together./Two drive it apart./Three
televisions bring on a war."

(Left to right) Karen Swenson, Bill Zavatsky, Tony Towle, and
Charles North are among the poets in the crowd demonstrating
their appreciation.

Pierre Martory

Pierre Martory was born in Bayonne in Southwest France, of partly Basque ancestry, and spent most of his childhood in Morocco. He received his *baccalauréat* in Bayonne and in 1939 enrolled at the School of Political Sciences in Paris. In June 1940 he took the last train to leave Paris before the Germans arrived; he returned after the war ended. For twenty-five years he wrote articles on music and theater for *Paris Match*, a weekly newsmagazine. His only published novel, *Phébus ou le beau mariage*, appeared in 1953. A collection of poems, *The Landscape Is Behind the Door* (Sheep Meadow Press, 1994), was translated by his longtime friend John Ashbery. The French edition of this collection marked the first time Martory's poems were published in his native country. Ashbery read his work at KGB on May 4, 1998, because Martory was then too ill to travel to the States. He died in the autumn of 1998.

BLUES

The bed of the railway links me to these days of hell
The bed of the railway just one night can do it all

Love of the others you wear me out with great strokes of a stiff brush

In a station of Paris is there a true love that smiles?
In a station of Paris everything begins and everything fails.

Love of the others you suck the young blood of my life

And the words of my big brother I still hear them on my cot
And the words of my big brother can it be he forgot?

Love of the others you are slow to promise a reward

So be it my child some people are never satisfied
So be it my child some win some fall by the wayside

Love of the others you put out my eyes by dint of fevers.

Goodbye is a big handkerchief a big handkerchief of paper
That you throw in the sewer once it's been spoiled with tears

Love of the others you leave in my mouth a taste of clay.

TRANSLATED BY JOHN ASHBERY

Donna Masini

Donna Masini's book of poems, *That Kind of Danger*, won the Barnard Women Poet's Prize in 1994 and was published by Beacon Press. Her novel, *About Yvonne*, was published by Norton and has just been released as a Penguin paperback. She is at work on her next collection of poems, to be published by Norton. She has received fellowships and grants from the National Endowment for the Arts and the New York Foundation for the Arts. Her poems have appeared in *The Paris Review*, *The Georgia Review*, *Parnassus*, and *Boulevard*. She is a professor of poetry at Hunter College and teaches writing workshops at Columbia University. She lives in New York City. She read at KGB on March 30, 1998.

TWO MEN, TWO GRAPEFRUITS

My husband made me juice—
each morning rose and in the kitchen,
in the early light idling through blue glass,
crushed the fruit, palmed it across
the juicer, filtered the pits and pulp and
carried it back to me, rubbing my shoulder
as I drank. My lover
rises early—hours before me—
slices the fruit and with a curved, serrated
knife, dissects each section, carefully separating
the membranes, as they say God first sliced
the person in two—man and woman—so that
each would ache for its other.

I want them both. I want the juice and the meat,
that pure exquisite liquid and the tender
flesh, the reddish pulp. All of us.
I don't know. If you get the pure juice, you lose
the juicy flesh and if you eat the flesh you miss
the way the juice goes down. So easily.

*Donna Masini relaxes during the intermission of her KGB reading. Donna
read poems of romantic adventure about "moving out of a marriage and
into a sublet downtown."*

J. D. McClatchy

J. D. McClatchy was born in Bryn Mawr, Pennsylvania, in 1945. He is the author of four books of poems, *Scenes from Another Life* (1981), *Stars Principal* (1986), *The Rest of the Way* (1990), and *Ten Commandments* (Knopf, 1998), and two collections of essays, *White Paper* (1990) and *Twenty Questions* (1998). He has edited many other books, including *The Vintage Book of Contemporary World Poetry* (1996), and written opera libretti for several composers. He is a chancellor of the Academy of American Poets and since 1991 has been the editor of *The Yale Review*. He wrote "Bishop Reading" for this anthology. He read at KGB on May 19, 1997.

BISHOP READING

And when she'd finished—having smoothed out
A map of the world with her accountant's voice,
Fresh paint on its creases, and towns dotted
With wine-glass elms, their distances lengthened
By mention of Boston terriers and Irish maids,
A rent-controlled rendezvous or rainstorm
Whose residue of mildew and leaves collected
Contentedly in the heart of a small-breasted friend—

I rushed backstage to gush. She looked me in the eye
With that sour authority reserved for the unknown
And snapped: "Go get my watch. I left it out there."
I nodded and walked out to stand for a moment

At the lectern where (but first I retrieved the watch,
Its face too small to read, its golden band
Minute enough for any camel to pass through)
She had just given us all the lives of our time.

Honor Moore

Honor Moore is the author of *The White Blackbird: A Life of the Painter Margarett Sargent by Her Granddaughter, Memoir* (poems), and *Mourning Pictures* (play). She lives in Connecticut and has published her work in *The Paris Review*, *The New Yorker*, and *The Nation*. She read at KGB on April 6, 1998.

A WINDOW AT KEY WEST

Waking in silence and, through tilted blinds,
the mark of red bougainvillea—pink light tossed
    at a white door. Out of sleep, I turn
in a narrow bed, and the sheet tugs after me.
    Walls the color of milk, wind dragging leaves
        across the courtyard, scraping whispers.
    Life is incomprehensible, he'd said
    when I asked if he had a theory. Late
        dalliance of tropical green,
bromeliad, look of palm bark, and beyond

    closed windows, a table set for supper.
In my dream I knock. A woman offers spoiled food
        then turns away. Now the sky goes dark
and the breeze stops. Why does she ask for narrative?
    You make plans but sit instead on a porch
        talking about Nietzsche whom you have
    never read—never has sense seemed less

consequential. His skin is very black
    against the white chair, his voice honest
and loose in the temperate air. The children

    ask to walk, but we sink into the large car,
drive the quiet, small streets of an old town. This is
      the shape my life takes around absence
any understanding would flatten. Light in the room,
    but the sound is blocked—all that suggests it
      is movement of light, shadow
    rippling a surface of tawny wicker.
    There are certain sentences I can't bear
      to speak again: *I can love you less.*
Of course I understand. He brings plates of food—

    green, then red, yellow. A red biplane, tall
glasses for beer, murmurs near a bar in shadow,
      greeting without handshake or embrace;
then today in a room on the ocean, late silver
    light, each chair a distinct bright color. He
    asks only for the present: her face
    behind a language I don't speak, something
    pulling. Beyond a closed window the noise
      of bodies in water, broken
by the talk of children. Her voice in this room

    waylays almost any grief. Standing there
at an ironing board, the dress patterned and torn,
    she burns her wrist: And so there will be

evidence. Later, wind and a raw Sunday heat: whites

go whiter, blacks blacken and glare until

eclipsed stripes of blind give actual

seconds of joy: red bougainvillea

late light flushes almost blue, blossoms

folded to the shape of bells so

brilliant now, they seem to tremble and ring out.

First time I was in KGB all crowded, could hardly find a seat, immediately wanted to read there, which I managed to do: The feel of the room brought back my poet youth in the seventies, when there was a Saturday afternoon series run by the indomitable Marguerite Harris (who began to write poems at about seventy) at a bar called Dr. Generosity's at Seventy-second Street and Second Avenue: that same rush-hour ambience and who's-who excitement and an equivalently imaginative combining of poets: I remember Erica Jong (then an up-and-coming versifier) reading with Yehuda Amichai (already Israel's greatest). What Dr. G with its sawdust floor lacked, KGB's hammer-and-sickle decor, which now (unlike then) we find so camp and reassuring, supplies . . .

HONOR MOORE

A secret message from Cavalier poet Richard Lovelace: "I could not love thee, dear, so much/Loved I not Honor Moore" (center). In left background, Ann Lauterbach chats with John Ashbery and David Lehman.

Melvin Jules Bukiet, part owner of KGB, has published several novels, including, most recently, the critically acclaimed Signs and Wonders.

Paul Muldoon

Paul Muldoon was born in Northern Ireland in 1951 and is now a citizen of the United States. He lives with his wife and daughter near Princeton, New Jersey, where he is Howard G. B. Clark Professor at Princeton University. His most recent books, from Farrar, Straus and Giroux, are *Hay* and *The Annals of Chile*, which was awarded the T. S. Eliot Prize. He read at KGB on September 29, 1997.

HARD DRIVE

With my back to the wall
and a foot in the door
and my shoulder to the wheel
I would drive through Seskinore.

With an ear to the ground
and my neck on the block
I would tend to my wound
in Belleek and Bellanaleck.

With a toe in the water
and a nose for trouble
and an eye to the future
I would drive through Derryfubble

and Dunnamanagh and Ballynascreen,
keeping that wound green.

Eileen Myles

Eileen Myles was born in Cambridge, Massachusetts. She lives in New York and Provincetown, and just finished her first novel, *Cool for You*. Her books include *School of Fish*, which won a 1998 Lambda Book Award, *Maxfield Parrish/early & new poems* (1995), *Chelsea Girls* (fiction, 1994), and *Not Me* (1991). With Liz Kotz she edited *The New Fuck You/adventures in lesbian reading* (Semiotext(e), 1995). She read at KGB on March 23, 1998.

MILK

I flew into New York
and the season
changed
a giant burr
something hot was moving
through the City
that I knew
so well. On the
plane though it was
white and stormy
faceless
I saw the sun
& remembered the warning
in the kitchen
of all places
in which I was

informed my wax
would melt
no one had gone high
around me,
where's the fear
I asked the
Sun. The birds
are out there
in their scattered
cheep. The people
in New York
like a tiny chain
gang are connected
in their
knowing
and their saving
one another. The
morning trucks
growl. Oh

save me from
knowing myself
if inside
I only melt.

About ten years ago I read in a group reading at a theater in San Francisco, the Victoria, in the Mission. It was a lesbian poetry reading, an event related to the Outwrite Conference, which was the first and definitely liveliest of a series of annual gay and lesbian literary conferences that began that year. I remember reading with Dorothy Allison, Chrystos, Marilyn Hacker—there were about seven of us and the place was packed. A deeply attentive audience.

I often recited my work at that time. It seemed performance had stolen poetry's thunder in the eighties, so in reciting my poems I slid a little bit into the turf of performance, and performing was particularly effective on nights like this with a wired audience that wanted to whoop it up. The poem I read (from my mind) was called "To the Maiden of Choice," and it was kind of an anti–new age tirade, though mainly it was riffing on the notion that one "chooses" one's life—this creepy theory included the notion of "choosing" disease and even AIDS, which I found hard to believe anyone "chose."

So in my poem I played with the idea that one even chose *one's parents,* and I speculated that "you/could have picked/the worst parents/on earth, say/Mr. & Mrs. William/F. Buckley—." And at this the crowd cheered and hooted. Buckley was a notorious homophobe who had just suggested HIV-positive people be tattooed on their butts for public safety. I accepted the laughs and the applause when my reading was over, and I was strolling through the lobby of the theater when yet another smiling woman came up to say she enjoyed my work. She wore glasses and had short blondish brown hair. "I've got to tell you something," she said. "I am the daughter of Pat and Bill Buckley." I was floored. And it had to be true, she looked like them. I felt like I manifested her. I began to apologize, awkwardly. After all, he was her *dad.* "It's okay," she said. "But they were *great.*" She gave me a big smile and walked away.

I always tell this story, to students or if there's a Q and A after a reading. It's my answer to the question Are poems true? Yes. More than we ever know.

EILEEN MYLES

Poet Eileen Myles and painter Bill Sullivan look as though they parked their Harleys out front. The latter inspired the former to write "Sullivan's Brain": "I left the ghetto/I'm standing way out/the black & the prongs of light/surrounding me/doodling in Nature/There is no one/on my beach."

Marie Ponsot read at KGB two weeks after winning the National Book Critics Circle Award for poetry.

Charles North

Charles North was born in New York City in 1941. He is the author of
seven collections of poetry, including *The Year of the Olive Oil* (Hang-
ing Loose Press, 1989) and *New and Selected Poems* (forthcoming from
Sun & Moon). His *No Other Way: Selected Prose* was published by
Hanging Loose in 1999. He is poet in residence at Pace University. He
read at KGB on March 2, 1998.

PHILOSOPHICAL SONGS

1. SOME OF THEM THAT DO FISH WILL GO FOR A MIDNIGHT SWIM

It's not so much the partis pris as
the performance which is then called into question.
Then back to the dents. Embrace of atmosphere

which isn't the wind that collects on the windowpane,
the word skidding dispassionately by way of
your gown of powder blue light. The cedars slip.

2. AS MOONLIGHT BECOMES YOU

refining the swale for the sake of
ordinary life, which isn't orderly
but does undergo a pattern of resolute change
because you supply the necessity: hence

ordinary life which isn't orderly,

marches on ahead into a swirl of reddening leaves

because you supply the necessity. Hence

the moon is rampant, flitting between you.

3. MADRIGAL

Not border or pass—not quite

    past either, post? postern? as

in the past reaching around its

turquoise plinth despite a coating of melted pine needles

or are they melting meanwhile the landscape has turned

    arrow-like to waste.

Distant squawks and pained foothills

not painted, not *intricately*

personal at best. Yet a morsel

off the top of a silo, flung from a train

closer than phenomenology more rapid than song

I know how it must sound, but my best reading experience, as I think about it, was at KGB last March with Eugene Richie. Despite all the smoke and the noise from outside, the presence in such intimate proximity of so many poets I admire made it feel as though the audience were a giant, ideal ("star-infested") ear, hearing absolutely everything I wanted them to hear and more. It was exhilarating. I contrast this with my recurrent nightmare reading: being up there with a black binder filled with poems I've never seen before and trying desperately to think of something to say, anything.

CHARLES NORTH

Charles North flanked by two generations of Hershons, the poet Bob (right), who is publisher of Hanging Loose Press, and Jed.

Deborah Garrison proving that a working girl can win: her book of poems was a smash hit in 1998.

Geoffrey O'Brien

Geoffrey O'Brien was born in New York City in 1948. His poetry has been collected in *A Book of Maps* (1989), *The Hudson Mystery* (1994), and *Floating City: Selected Poems 1978–1995* (1996). He is also the author of *Hardboiled America* (1981), *DreamTime: Chapters from the Sixties* (1988), *The Phantom Empire* (1993), *The Times Square Story* (1998), and *Bardic Deadlines: Reviewing Poetry, 1984–1995* (1998). He has contributed frequently to *The New York Review of Books* and *The Village Voice*, and was editor of *The Reader's Catalog* (1989). He is editor in chief of the Library of America, where he has worked since 1992. He read at KGB on November 24, 1997.

THE LAKE

1.

The lake
is shaped like wind.

2.

The body of it
persistent

as in the space
where a play was done
the arrangements of light.

3.

The rigged blooms
tied to their trellis,
the coils
and racks of filters.

Empty frame
where it happens.

4.

From the lake window
the wood noises came in
to say they went down
near the water
to gather the shapes of things.

5.

Gestures printed on air.

A spider-thread spiral
no longer inhabited by the gesturer.

6.

Like Chinese writing

it stoops down
where the breath starts

to stand in for grass.

7.

Five stalks
hesitant
in the black garden's
stubble carpet.

8.

To waver,
to be plucked,

to be twisted
pliable and grassy
out of rigor.

9.

Empty frame
where it happens.

The shadow players bent
one toward other
under suspended gauze.

A movement
as of stopped water.

10.

The lake
is shaped by wind.

11.

It uncurls in the cold.
All morning the furrows
repeat nothing.

12.

The tips of the furrows
seem to nestle
against what pushes them.

*Geoffrey O'Brien in an exceptionally good mood on the March day he
learned that he had won a Guggenheim Fellowship. The poet Marjorie
Welish helps him celebrate.*

Michael O'Brien

Michael O'Brien's *The Floor and the Breath* was published by Cairn Editions in 1994. His *Sills: Selected Poems* is forthcoming from Zoland Books. He read at KGB on March 16, 1998.

POEM

Little bones of
the ear, house built

of air, cloud-wraiths
cross hillside, wind

lays shadow on
water, leaf-shape

on wall, day bears
down, seamless, last

bird's slow song, a
pipe reversed, con-

stellation of
four tones, shifting

Molly Peacock

Molly Peacock was born in Buffalo, New York, in 1947. Her books of poems include *Original Love* (Norton, 1995) and *Take Heart* (Vintage, 1989). Her poems have appeared in *The New Yorker*, *The Paris Review*, *The Nation*, *The New Republic*, and *Poetry*. She is a contributing editor of *House & Garden* and the author of a prose memoir, *Paradise, Piece by Piece* (Riverhead, 1998). She read at KGB on April 21, 1997.

BREAKFAST WITH CATS

The advent of the new habit
occurred the day the cats
were ignoring us.
Falling in love
with my new electric frother,
I made café au lait
in lion size cups
as my husband perused "The Science *Times*."
Thus it was a Tuesday.
On Monday we had ignored them.
Deadlines to meet, of course.
Preclusive of petting;
nor had we made love.
Nor do we ever eat breakfast at a proper table.
We eat in the living room by the big window
so we can hear every decibel
of the buses' brakes' bellows' breath below
where the East Village spreads out in blocks & streets

like the wheat field squares & apple orchard rows
our cats would roam in—if not
for that word "like."
In my enthusiasm for the slender white frother,
I overfrothed.

Feeling the deep silence of our cats
in their berths beneath the tablecloth
I put the extra froth in two
blue and white bowls
which had reproached us
with their tiny emptinesses
since we had purchased them in Chinatown
never thinking of a single thing that could go in them
because we had only solid thoughts.
The milk was a liquid thought.

When the room's reds reddened as in a Flemish painting,
richer because the sun went in
as it began to rain lightly and gently on the East Village
the buses' moist brakes breathing
more deeply as they came to their sensible safe stops,
I placed the tiny bowls
by my footstool.
My lounging husband looked up in alertness
too feral merely to hold a cup.
After the two cats' heads appeared delicately
around the sides of the wing backed chair,
they lowered their triangle chins into their bowls
at the left

and at the right
and had their fill
circled the carpet medallion
then lay in the lower ocean of the room,
their habit become a habit
in a right instance.
And every morning since they have each sat
in the original positions of the bowls
waiting for their froth.
It is froth for which gods live.

I dare not count the numbers of establishment poetry readings I have attended with a terrible physical expectancy of claustrophobia despite the airiness of those chandeliered, high-ceilinged rooms. With clenched heart muscles I have waited as both men and women, boys and girls, have shuffled papers in a distraction at a podium that can come only from being so deeply inside themselves that we the audience are nothing, nothing . . . and heard them saying vaporously, "Do I still have time?" The polite answer to this fascist question always seems to be yes.

And yet.

At KGB in the stifling red room there is little posturing. The reading series is so distinguished that major writers kill to be asked—for free with no book sales whatever—by the ingenious duo of David Lehman and Star Black, whose zesty pairing of poets with interlocking poetics always provides an aesthetic snap. Everything about the shabby place holds the vicious honesty of art passionately made, so poets behave themselves in an uncommon luxury of self-awareness and even kindness toward an audience so discriminating that it selects second by second the true from the false step. Nothing is fake here, except perhaps the small deception that Lehman's martini glass contains not the famous vodka of the bar but mineral water.

MOLLY PEACOCK

In London's Poetry Review *the critic Stephen Burt wrote that Liam Rector, pictured here on the night of his KGB reading in February 1999, was a leader of a group of poets Burt called the "ellipticals." Introducing Liam, David Lehman couldn't resist commenting that "he is unpredictable, far from your typical elliptical, often heretical, perhaps historical. In short, in matters skeptical, poetical, hysterical, he is the very model of a modern major elliptical."*

"If New York City is a party and poetry is life, here is the life of the party. Ladies and gentlemen, John Ashbery."

Wang Ping

Wang Ping was born in Shanghai and came to the United States in 1985. Her books include *American Visa* (short stories), *Foreign Devil* (a novel), and *Of Flesh and Spirit* (poems). Her anthology of contemporary Chinese poetry is forthcoming from Hanging Loose Press. She read at KGB on April 7, 1997.

FROM "RAIN, CLOUDS, EIGHT THOUSAND MILES OF ROADS"

In Memory of Allen

No cloud or rain all night long.
Before the dawn broke, you strolled in again,
smiling, your face peaceful after three hours chanting.
You listened to my babbling, my painful effort to bring out
those faces from the High Land, but words fail when it comes
to the unspeakable, my stories only phantoms of memory.
Once again you took my hand and pressed it to your lips.
You were also planning a trip to Tibet with a group of
friends, you said, but your doctor worried about your heart.
I gazed into your eyes—where mist formed
like wild horses, like stormy clouds running
from peak to peak along the Himalayan Range—
energy that overflows its form and has to spend itself
—like your love, how you've loved this city and its people,
fractured and screwed up as it is, your love with such
intensity that it traveled eight thousand miles through clouds
and rain until it reached Tibet at the speed of light . . .

How strange to see your face everywhere
as I walked down Second Avenue for the season's
last reading at St. Mark's Church—your face
on every trembling leaf in the late spring breeze, faces
of the dying in the light of a crescent moon
against abandoned walls, faces of Jersey
kids sticking their fat cheeks out of the sun roof
of the rental limousine screaming in ecstasy, old man
shoving his fist into his mouth to stifle a sob—
face of the rock
that measures 29,028 feet, the river of stars
splashing across the indigo face of the night
on the last day of May through wind and forest—
your face illuminated with a fire that swells from the gut—
your shirt, scarf, buttons, your hands,
arms, waist, thighs, all flying in different directions
in the heat of joy, not about air but earth,
about sinking—to the very bottom—where all is made of
the same substance—then something will happen—
a transformation from inside, a sunflower bursting . . .

You've been with us,
coming and going in the form of flesh and blood, your body
besieged by the solemn, sad, angry faces of death,
your life a long preparation, a journey to the source.
We've been sleeping in time's hungry grip;
now you wake, having tossed away things, possessions,
knowledge, logic, to enter the soundless
   —the original call of all things.

Our remembrance, and yours,
all taken by the ocean, all given—
Your death is not a void,
 but love boundless.

The bird has finally reached its nest
 in the sun—the key is hidden
 in the sunlight
  at the window.

May 29, 1997, Astor Place, Manhattan
May 30, 1997, Brooklyn

Reading Nightmares

Chicago Guild Complex: Flew all the way there from New York to give a reading. But every address my contact person gave me was wrong. It was a deadly cold windy day in February. I roamed around downtown Chicago for eight hours trying to find the place where I was supposed to read. It was called the Hot House.

Barnes & Noble: My first time reading for *The Best American Poetry.* I was given ten minutes maximum, but I went on for half an hour.

Museum of Modern Art: My first gig ever, translating for Allen Ginsberg, Gary Snyder, and the Chinese Misty School poets. When I got up, I couldn't say a word except shouting my own name repeatedly into the microphone.

Bronx Museum: I read my funniest poems, including the one with many curses, but no one laughed.

WANG PING

Robert Polito

Robert Polito was born in Boston in 1951 and educated at Boston College and Harvard University. He is the author of a collection of poems, *Doubles* (University of Chicago Press), and *Savage Art* (Knopf), a biography of the pulp novelist Jim Thompson, which won the National Book Critics Circle and Edgar Awards in criticism in 1996. He directs the M.F.A. writing program at New School University. He recently received a Guggenheim Fellowship. He read at KGB on February 10, 1997.

OVERHEARD IN THE LOVE HOTEL

Again the cab slips west down 14th almost
To the river—
The cobbled meat market, steel grates down;
A thrown-up Christmas tree
Lot on an old dock beyond the stalled highway;
A whiff of blood and the first snow
That keeps not falling.

We've just checked into the Love Hotel—
Film noir signatures on the register:
"Tom Neal," "Ann Savage";
Spouses discarded, even her
Two other lovers forsaken at the bolted door.

Fading polyester roses drape the bed—matching
Trellis on an overhead mirror; evening breeze
Out of Hoboken through cracked panes
—Nothing can dispel the half-life traces of Roach Bomb
She chases with a blunt cigar . . .
"So sexy you brought these. This is sweet—
And throws a little curve into the day."

Blue ice pail; Absolut from a frosted cup.
Raking her new coil of brassy curls,
"Can you picture me with grey hair?
My mother passed her forties as a blonde;
Now you know my true color—

You and a few others."
Wrapping her ankles around his, she pins
Him on the spread
As from a room upstairs springs rattle to a finish;
"It's like I'm one of them . . .
All the passion, the ecstasy—
We spend the rest of our lives trying to shake."

Reflected along the ceiling, freckles
From her back rotate constellations
He traces like a blind man reading a star map;
"You've got to see who I am—
These yearnings, sometimes they last two years,

Or they can burn out after all of seven seconds;
But they're intense, and very real."
The wall phone rings—*Twenty minutes, please.*
"I wish I could say I didn't know
How they call just before your time's up,
Or not getting your hair wet in the shower,
The towels that irritate your skin"—

Six-inch scar across her panty-line
Where last spring the surgeon
Scooped out her insides,
Reddening with soap and steam;
And still stings when she wears silk.

Outside, snow holding. Another cab.
"Where was I, tonight? I've been
Lying to Kevin about Steve, Steve about Kevin;
And to Stanley about both of them . . .
Only you have the whole story.
First time I lie to you—
Then you'll know we're really going someplace."

Katha Pollitt

Katha Pollitt was born in New York City in 1949. A graduate of Radcliffe College, she is the author of *Antarctic Traveller* (Knopf, 1982), which won the National Book Critics Circle Award in poetry. She has also received awards from the Guggenheim Foundation and the National Endowment for the Arts, as well as a Fulbright Fellowship. She is an associate editor of *The Nation*. Some of her columns from *The Nation* were published by Knopf in a collection entitled *Reasonable Creatures* in 1994. She read at KGB on March 24, 1997.

MIND-BODY PROBLEM

When I think of my youth I feel sorry not for myself
but for my body. It was so direct
and simple, so rational in its desires,
wanting to be touched the way an otter
loves water, the way a giraffe
wants to amble the edge of the forest, nuzzling
the tender leaves at the tops of the trees. It seems
unfair, somehow, that my body had to suffer
because I, by which I mean my mind, was saddled
with certain unfortunate high-minded romantic notions
that made me tyrannize and patronize it
like a cruel medieval baron, or an ambitious
English-professor husband ashamed of his wife—
her love of sad movies, her budget casseroles
and regional vowels. Perhaps

my body would have liked to make some of our dates,
to come home at four in the morning and answer my scowl
with "None of your business!" Perhaps
it would have liked more presents: silks, mascaras.
If we had had a more democratic arrangement
we might even have come, despite our different backgrounds,
to a grudging respect for each other, like Tony Curtis
and Sidney Poitier fleeing handcuffed together
instead of the current curious shift of power
in which I find I am being reluctantly
dragged along by my body as though by some
swift and powerful dog. How eagerly
it plunges ahead, not stopping for anything,
as though it knows exactly where we are going.

The best thing that ever happened to me at a poetry reading was hearing Elizabeth Bishop read her poetry at the Guggenheim Museum in the 1970s. Miss Bishop had let me audit her poetry class my senior year in college and I admired her enormously. I know there are those who say she wasn't a very good teacher, but I thought she was wonderful—sane, down-to-earth, playful, kind. People also say she was very shy, but I must say she did not strike me this way—perhaps because I was so in awe of her that I was rather shy in her presence myself. In any case, I had heard that Miss Bishop was a terrible reader of her own poetry—flat, dull, withdrawn, nervous, just reading the poems in a straightforward prosy way one after the other without a lot of fireworks or drama, such as one got at a reading by Lowell, or Bly, or Sexton. But she came out, with her tidy gray hair and her conservative wool suit, and she read her poems in a pleasant, conversational way and it was all fine. I decided, sitting there, that there can be no such thing as a poet who is a bad reader of his or her own writing, because only the poet can give you the unique experience of hearing the writer read the work. Thus, by definition, the poet's reading is neither good nor bad but, rather, expressive of that person, and there is no reason ever to be nervous when reading your poems in front of an audience! Short of falling down drunk or bursting into tears, it can't go wrong, because however you read is what people came to hear. This conviction (along with a secret belief that most people in the audience aren't paying attention anyway) made it possible for me to avoid performance anxiety. Because there was no longer a performance: there was just me.

Unfortunately, this insight may be connected with the worst things that have ever happened to me at a poetry reading. For some reason—because I am short? female? lacking in personal dignity?—a number of notable poets have felt, over the years, the need to come up to me after I've given a reading and critique my diction, my verbal habits, my way of introducing each poem. I suppose I should be grateful that they don't take the poems apart as well, but it is surprisingly upsetting to be told by a colleague—invariably a rather older colleague, but still—not to say "um," or that one has a "girlish voice," or that one makes too many humorous remarks between the poems. I suppose I could try out on these people my theory that the poet can do no wrong in reading her own work, but, as so often, one only thinks of these things later.

KATHA POLLITT

Anne Porter

Anne Porter was born in Sherborn, Massachusetts, in 1911. In 1932 she married the painter Fairfield Porter, with whom she had five children. Her collection, *An Altogether Different Language: Poems, 1934–1994*, was published by Zoland Books in 1994 and was short-listed for the National Book Award in poetry that year. A version of "Five Wishes" appeared in *Commonweal* and was subsequently revised. Anne Porter read at KGB on December 15, 1997.

Anne Porter in the luminous light that her poems seem to inspire.

FIVE WISHES

I'd like to have a wild bird
Perch on my hand
Perhaps a sparrow or
A chickadee
Sudden with her sharp feet
And fragile daring

I'd like to see again
The etchings Rembrandt made
Of stories from the Bible

Though they're as plain
As Bethlehem's hay
A homely radiance fills them

And I would like to visit
The Laguna Indians
In their adobe villages
And their small ancient church
That's made of whitewashed clay
With logs for rafters

And in it their Madonna
To whom they've given
An apron of white lace

And I would like to learn
How to accept my death
To accept our dying

That strange dawn
Which is so deeply scandalous
That God himself wept
At the death of his friend

And I would like to find
The little shrine of Chimayó
Where the lame leave their crutches

I'd like to go there
With my daughter Katie

And it would be enough
Just to be there
Without any miracle.

Anna Rabinowitz

Anna Rabinowitz's first collection of poetry, *At the Site of Inside Out* (University of Massachusetts Press), won the Juniper Prize. Her work has appeared widely in journals such as *The Atlantic Monthly*, *The Paris Review*, *Colorado Review*, *Denver Quarterly*, and *New American Writing*, and in the anthologies *The Best American Poetry 1989* and *Life on the Line: Selections on Words and Healing*. She edits *American Letters and Commentary*. She read at KGB on April 14, 1997.

OF JOY ILLIMITED: POLYPHONIC SOUNDINGS: SHORE TO SHIP

Owned by a heat:—*There is something in my heart like a burning Fire—*
    shut up in my bones—hear me, hear me—

Joyless in these loitering hours—bring silver spoons, a down quilt,
    a photo of our house—I have fevered for thee
On Orchard Street, on Delancey, on Grand—*and I am weary with*
    holding it in—and I cannot—this burning churning—

Yes—oh, yes—stream unto me, into me—I will marcell
    my hair, rouge my cheeks, moisten my lips—
I will put a new song in my mouth—I will plant high trees
    in your ear—

Latebloomers rally to light—*pent up in my bones*—I will
    filigree air—
Like a burning fire—roaring in flight—come quickly from the ship—

I will co-sign your flank, I will ghostwrite your loins—
My heart, lynx-eye of hope—bring a silk blouse blazing with
    rose, a wool scarf lusty with green—

I am weary with holding it in—and I cannot—if my fever-tongue knew
    how to speak—
There is something in my heart—bring opera glasses, a coral brooch,
    buttons wild with bone—

Engulfed by this heat—swollen—flaring—this waiting thickened,
    brambled with heat—
Do you hear me—*locked up in my bones*—will you know me—
    shall I row to you, flame to your boat—

Carter Ratcliff

Carter Ratcliff's books of poetry include *Fever Coast* and *Give Me Tomorrow*. His forthcoming collection is entitled *Sluggo in Love*. *The Fate of a Gesture: Jackson Pollock and Postwar American Art*, his most recent nonfiction book, was published by Farrar, Straus and Giroux in 1996. He has published books and essays on art in the United States and Europe, and is a contributing editor of *Art in America*. He read at KGB on February 24, 1997.

THE BIG BAD ART THING

They would ask him,
what is the secret.
What is the secret
of your success, and
He would tell them,
I stay away.
I stay very far away,
away from the big bad art thing

It's white
and it's a powder
It's red
and it's a liquid
It's green.
It's got liquidity.

Well, that sounds good.

He'd say, it does.
It sounds quite good.
Liquidity is always good
In principle. In fact,
it flows from wounds

you had before
you even heard
of art and now

we've let the secret
get away because
We let ourselves
get far too close,
too close
to the big bad art thing.

Well, I agree because
My mother made a video
Of me at the beach
Being born

It's a beautiful film

But you know sometimes
I worry about mom
Sometimes I'm afraid

She got too close,
too close to the
big bad art thing.

It made those wounds
then flowed away
down these stairwells
and into books.

It left this stain.
It's green. It cast
this shadow.

And it's white,
it dried the mucous membranes.

They shrivel up
and blow away, very
far away.

Cartilage collapses
The remnant is a ruin
It's picturesque. It's
Mathew Brady, Richmond,
Virginia, after the bombardment.
Albumin print, eighteen-sixty
-three-sixty-five,
six and one half by
eight and one-quarter

inches. Museum
of Modern Art, New York.

It's black and it's a concept
It's white and it's a fluid
It's green and it's a texture

It's wide and it's utopian.
It's calm and I
feel fine,

but you know, sometimes,
I feel afraid.
I feel a slippage
in the red, and very

far from red, it's
a cypress tree, it's
Barnett Newman, Death
of Euclid, nineteen
-forty-seven, oil
on canvas, six
-teen by twenty
inches, Anonymous
Promised Gift,
National
Gallery of Art,
Washington, D.C.

It's green and now
it's night. It's far
away. You get
there on a boat,
and it is solid as a rock.
It's shiftier than sand.

And sometimes I'm afraid

I built my house
too close by far,
too close to the
big bad art thing.
It's red and it's a shadow.
It's white and sinks in water.

It flows away, far
away, but he thinks
it stays. He's all confused.
He thinks he's found a friend.
It's Caravaggio, Narcissus,
oil on canvas, forty
-three and five six
-teenths by thirty
-six and one quarter
inches, one-hundred
and ten by ninety-two
centimeters, Galeria
Nazionale d'Arte

Antica, Palazzo
Corsini, Rome. He's

sinking in
the image. He's
flowing far away. It's
about identity and
then again, it's
not. It is and it
isn't, and so if I
were you—because
it really is
about identity, and

sometimes I'm afraid
it's not a Caravaggio.
Or he is not Narcissus, or
he is and he can't tell,
and do you know why?

Because he got, he got
too close, oh far too
close, too close to the
big bad art thing.

Because it's cognitive.
And it's expressive, too.
It's larger than life
But smaller than death.

So stay away, stay
far away, far
away from the
big bad art thing.

At my first poetry reading, on February 4, 1968, I met a woman named
Phyllis Derfner, and, Reader, I married her.

CARTER RATCLIFF

Victoria Redel

Victoria Redel's collection of poems *Already the World* (Kent State University Press, 1995) won the Stan and Tom Wick Prize. She also has a collection of stories, *Where the Road Bottoms Out* (Knopf, 1995). She teaches at Sarah Lawrence College and in the Vermont College M.F.A. program. She read at KGB on March 3, 1997.

SINGING TO TONY BENNETT'S COCK

Does it really matter, really, if it's true or not,
but just, really, to think of it, Tony Bennett's cock
in his hotel room at the San Juan Americana
while Rosario knelt over it, her mouth brushing over it,
her crooning, "Ladies and Gentlemen,
here tonight, straight from six sold-out weeks
at the fabulous, the world-famous Atlantic City's Taj Mahal
is the one, the only, Mister Tony Bennett."
And with that she'd sing, tilting and leaning into
the purpled head, all the old Tony Bennett classics
and for an encore some new songs
she'd make up for him on the spot.
What if it is true, really? What if I told you Rosario is a twin—
would that stretch your belief?
That they dance flamenco in separate cities?
That they are over fifty? That the sister's name means hope?
Are you with me still? Are you really ready to know
that all Tony Bennett wanted was to go down on her,

that she claims that after coming

her mouth goes cold as marble? She has lost me

with this intrusion of marble, and I don't want to lose you.

It's just her claim, after all. I have heard a woman claim

that she didn't like it, a man's mouth on her,

or women who will not take a man in their mouths,

let alone to sing the cock, sing the cock, sing the cock,

and other women, still, exhausted by claims.

I want none of it, I want it all, your castanet heart,

your secrets walking around naked, a rash of honesty,

your raucous coming, not stilled. Does the twin's mouth

marble too? The San Juan Americana, that sounds

good enough to me. And for you, can we say love?

Can we say he went there thirsting her ochre menses

and came up smeary and beyond any backyard Gods.

Tell me, really, Tony, is it true—ochred or purpled

or San Juan? How are the new classics?

In the next suite there is always a man on a phone

claiming, "I'm just the same in real life."

In the next to the next room, room service knocks twice.

The hotel charges fifty cents a call. *Can we say love?*

"Is that what you wanted?" he said. Plates and forks,

eggs and meat ransacked on the tray outside the door.

"Not till you went there," she said. "Now it's all I want."

Sometimes before giving a reading I find myself recalling the afternoon I stood up to give my high school graduation speech. I took a breath and began. After about the third sentence, my speech was interrupted by a woman shouting, "Louder! Louder! You must speak louder!" I didn't have to locate her in the audience to know it was my own mother shouting at me. Now before I give a reading, I imagine my mother, Natasha—dead fifteen years—and how if I don't speak up, she'll be yelling back into the living, "Louder! Louder!"

VICTORIA REDEL

Martha Rhodes

Martha Rhodes is the author of *At the Gate* (Provincetown Arts Press). Her poems have appeared in *Agni, American Poetry Review, Columbia, Harvard Review,* and *Ploughshares.* She teaches at Emerson College in Boston and at the New School for Social Research in New York. She is the director of Four Way Books, an independent literary press. She read at KGB on December 1, 1997.

IT BEING FORBIDDEN

to excuse oneself from table
before each morsel is chewed and swallowed;
it being forbidden to laugh
unless he conducts, pitch and duration,
his arms raised, our sisterly heads shamed
downward; it being forbidden
to invite another to that table who dares
to be more handsome and charming than he.

It being commanded to worship
that occupier of the armed-chair,
carver of pheasants, rabbinic imposter,
tweed-suited weekend gardener,
peddler of diamonds to the ghetto

and we do worship him
for plentiful is his table,

joyous the summer camps,
vast the Canadian forests,
the Caribbean Sea.

He who orchestrates with knife and fork
pulls us to our knees
and we pray with him who whispers
do you love me
and we cry with him who whimpers
no one loves me
and we kiss him on his temple
no one touches me
and we remain in his house
longer than we ought, for he prophesies
even you shall leave me
and when we do leave him, as we must,
we transplant lilacs and peonies from his garden
to ours so that he shall bloom
beneath our windows.

The first reading that I gave and even attended was when I was sixteen, in Boston, at a Boston Arts Festival event, as part of a poetry workshop which I thought was just a poetry workshop. My group was lined up onstage, African drum players began drumming, and we were announced as P (drum, drum) R (drum, drum) I (drumdrum) S (Drumdrumdrum) M drumdrumdrumdrum PRISM Post Revolutionary Indigenous Scribblers Movement PRISM!!!!!!!!!!!!!!!!! One of the drummers took me aside—"You could use a hit of this"—and I took a toke off a fifteen-pound joint and passed out. . . . 1970-something at The Cedar, screwed through a two-hour open mike in the ladies' room stall with some guy whose name begins a Hebrew prayer. . . . St. Mark's Church Robert Lowell booed off the stage, drunk, his papers falling off the podium, slurring, Ginsberg trying to help him, people shouting at Lowell, "Get off the fucking stage, asshole." . . . What I thought was going to be a radio show interview/short reading for a Baltimore area show (in a small studio) turned out to be a live variety show (five-hundred-plus audience) with burlesque and skits about nurses. The announcer: Next, we have a live poet. . . . I see London, I see France, I see Martha Rhodes's underpants! (live orchestra, theme song from *M*A*S*H* as I walk on the stage). . . . Hellloooo, Martha! A real live poet, folks, reading her real live poems, right, Martha? They're sad, they're funny, they're a dime a rhyme (theme song from *Cheers*) . . .

MARTHA RHODES

Martha Rhodes (left)—shown here with her friend Susan Abraham— directs Four Way Books and founded the CCS reading series at the Civic Center Synagogue on White Street in Tribeca.

Eugene Richie

Eugene Richie has published two poetry collections, *Island Light* (Painted Leaf Press, 1998) and *Moiré* (Groundwater Press, 1989). With Edith Grossman he cotranslated *My Night with Federico García Lorca* (Painted Leaf Press, 1997), a book of poems by Jaime Manrique. He teaches in the department of English and in the Masters of Science in Publishing Program at Pace University in New York. He read at KGB on March 2, 1998.

AIRPORTS OF THE WORLD

I think the train is headed this way,
right through those sliding doors and into this room.
The sound of splitting firewood is so near.
Red and black at the core and heaped
against the concrete building. It's unbelievable.
You feel like you're returning to the mire,
though this is definitely not
a case of the pot calling the kettle back.

Rome is like the center
for so many international organizations.
I saw only part of it. I walked around all day.
Fidel Castro was there. I spent a lot of time there.
Then I wanted to go to the Baths of Caracalla.
Carabinieri came up to me and said I couldn't.

There's nothing like seeing Paris covered in snow.
I checked in *The New York Times* in December—
sixteen days of rain. I wish
I could go to Paris again with Catalina.
First, I couldn't find it and finally I found it.
There's like a lot of action—music.
Saturday we had a tour of the city and then,
on our own. We spent a whole day at Versailles.
The outside is very beautiful,
with the fountains going all the time—
I mean some are, some aren't.
We saw Chopin's grave. That's incredible.

Did I tell you this guy Robert has a Web site?
I checked it out at work, but
Mitch's computer is not that great.
Hopefully, I'll get a Web page out of it.
Usually you get on the phone from another site.
That's not all there is.

If you're into anything about design,
Milan is the fashion center of the world.
I've been there twice. I know that place
backwards and forwards.
They're doubling the size of the airport.
Athens's airport is embarrassing. The lack of security—
you walk from the terminal out onto the tarmac.
They've started building another airport.
Kennedy is an architectural monument.

Part of La Guardia is new.
Oakland airport is beautiful.

Well, at least you can't accuse us
of throwing good water after bad.
Sometimes it needs a lot of watching—
it seems to go crazy now and then.
The film we wanted to see,
Roman Polanski's *Repulsion,*
is still in an airport warehouse in Ohio.

Hugh Seidman

Hugh Seidman was born in Brooklyn in 1940. His first book, *Collecting Evidence*, won the Yale Series of Younger Poets prize. He has been a recipient of fellowships from the New York Foundation for the Arts and the National Endowment for the Arts. His most recent collection is *Selected Poems: 1965–1995* (Miami University Press). He read at KGB on March 16, 1998.

GAIL

I am sixteen you are my first love.
Your breasts are small under yellow cashmere.

The plastic surgeon has smoothed your cheerleader's nose.

It is Sunday at your uncle's in Boro Park in Brooklyn.
The light of the heavens whitens the floor.

I am kissing you in the taste of cigarette, the odor of perfume.

I am sixteen and do not know
that I will never not remember this afternoon.

I am sixteen and do not imagine
how envy fails friendship
how anger thwarts love
how arrogance is humbled.

I am sixteen and do not recall
the dead behind the sky
trapped in the impenetrable.

I am sixteen and do not think
how you are each who turns away
how you are each from whom I will turn.

I am sixteen and can think of nothing
but the pungency of cigarette, the reek of perfume.

As you lean back in the smoke that swirls about your face.

Vijay Seshadri

Vijay Seshadri was born in India in 1954 and grew up in Columbus, Ohio. He attended Oberlin College and Columbia University's doctoral program in Middle Eastern studies. A collection of his poems, *Wild Kingdom*, was published in 1996 by Graywolf Press. He lives in Brooklyn with his wife and son, and earns his living as a magazine editor and freelance writer. He read at KGB on February 24, 1997.

THE SCHOLAR

Illusions she didn't know she had were shattered when
she saw in the text she was cleaning up—
the corrupt recension of the now lost text—
not the cypress of heaven
or the morphology of a recurring type
or the riverbank where a god dances
but her own self's circumstances,

and not in the lover but the miserable sinner
who, as the poem trembled
to the death of its god,
drew back in fear
and so came to be noticed
by the demon who so resembled
her sworn enemy in her department,
with his bleak chin and his knowing look.
Though prodded by him she did write the book

that captured it all—god, demon, lover, avatar,
the ascension by night, the great battle,
the sobbing behind the ruined lattice—
and suspended it between her mother tongues
in the cat's cradle of her scholarly apparatus—
made from shards, really, but mysteriously there.

David Shapiro

David Shapiro was born in Newark, New Jersey, in 1947. He is the au-
thor of many volumes of art criticism, translation and poetry, most re-
cently *After a Lost Original* (1994) and *House (Blown Apart)* (1988),
both from Overlook Press. He has received the Morton Dauwen Zabel
Prize from the American Academy of Arts and Letters as well as grants
from the National Endowment for the Arts and the Ingram Merrill
Foundation. He has taught widely, most recently at Bard College,
William Paterson College, and the Cooper Union. He read at KGB on
April 20, 1998.

OLD POEMS

Sinking, below the star-several harps
of evening, in one distant garden,
the new poem, twisted from the skin of the old whining birch—
Perhaps I am also dedicated to an angel's memory
her long black hair collected in my bed.
Now the youngest poet cries, I love countdowns! I love
the last few seconds of joy!
But the old poet knows the error in transcription
is correct: Nirvana is *some sorrow.*
Remember our last hacked Ariels
lie ruined in their melody. Two poems, folded, twisted together.
The earliest song: Because you have joined me
this great tree was felled. Is it worthless?
Because you have joined

never to leave again
spring has become the spring I had hoped for
and this crooked pebble is singing in the forest.
But the new poem, the winter flower, is not sweet.

The readings that meant the most to me were probably my father's voice as he recited in a great *fortissimo* the poems of Milton and Blake he loved. Then, family presentations of poems memorized like music. My father later took me to hear Theodore Roethke at the Ninety-second Street Y. Mrs. Florence Lennon put me on her show on WEVD when I was thirteen. In August 1962, I met Kenneth Koch and I loved his quiet way of reducing too grandiloquent stanzas. My astonishment two years later while hearing John Ashbery recite all of "The Skaters," my favorite poem of his, was the perfection of his white-on-white style. My son accompanied me in readings in Portugal and said: "How many people are we against tonight?" He wriggled a bit nervously when he recited at St. John the Divine in front of thousands: a peace poem for the Mideast. I was horrified to hear my own readings and those of many poets—I called readings the worst thing "in" nature. But I was fortunate when Allen Ginsberg read at Columbia with me and the windows were swarming with his admirers, and I saw tears in his eyes. I have been amazed to hear the voices of Ungaretti at Frank O'Hara's, and Frank's strange metallic voice at Columbia University. The truest voice I have heard was the rabbinical ecstasy of Meyer Schapiro on Cézanne and the philosophers. I loved the voice of my friend Joseph Ceravolo and his impossibly dry renditions. Overwhelmed by the bravery of Tory Dent, speaking of her struggles with sickness. The architect John Hejduk recently went to MIT and recited at an architectural lecture nothing but prayers. This is how readings—competitive, lugubrious, and meretricious often—can become something sacred, indelible, amazing, and alive.

DAVID SHAPIRO

David Shapiro describes himself in a recent poem ("After Poetry") as
"a Luddite with a laptop in his lap."

Harvey Shapiro

Harvey Shapiro has published ten books of poetry, the most recent of which is *Selected Poems* (Wesleyan University Press, 1997). He is a Rockefeller grantee in poetry and a Pushcart Prize winner. He works as a senior editor at *The New York Times Magazine* and was editor of *The New York Times Book Review* from 1975 to 1983. He read at KGB on April 6, 1997.

6/20/97

It's Friday night and I've just had
another helping of Ben & Jerry's coffee
fudge frozen yogurt because I saw
David Ignatow at Columbia-Presbyterian,
8th floor, Milstein, room 426, after a quick
ride on the skip 9, the one that does
every other stop, and David, who is
recovering from a stroke, doesn't look
too good, a transparent mask over
his face, feeding him oxygen, whiffs of
steam eddying from it, or maybe con
trails because David is going very fast,
talking to himself and jerking his body
violently. On the other hand, the view
from his window is splendid, the
lordly Hudson cloaked in late afternoon
sun. I say to the nurse, his color is good,

and she says, that's because we're giving
him blood, pointing to the tubing. Count
Dracula was right, she says, it
makes you look good.
But it's not for real.

Charles Simic

Charles Simic was born in Belgrade, Yugoslavia, in 1939 and emigrated to the United States in 1953. Since 1967 he has published more than sixty books in this country and abroad. His latest poetry collections are *Jackstraws*, *Walking the Black Cat*, and *A Wedding in Hell*, all from Harcourt Brace. In 1990 he won the Pulitzer Prize for *The World Doesn't End*, a collection of prose poems. He served as guest editor of *The Best American Poetry 1992*. His most recent book of prose is *Orphan Factory*, which was published in the University of Michigan's Poets on Poetry series in 1998. In 1984 he was awarded a MacArthur Fellowship. He lives in New Hampshire. He read at KGB on February 12, 1998.

THE LIVES OF ALCHEMISTS

The great labor was always to efface oneself,
Reappear as something entirely different:
The pillow of a young woman in love,
A ball of lint pretending to be a spider.

Black boredoms of rainy country nights
Thumbing the writings of illustrious adepts
Offering advice on how to proceed with the transmutation
Of a figment of time into eternity.
The true master, one of them counseled,
Needs a hundred years to perfect his art

In the meantime, the small arcana of the frying pan,
The smell of olive oil and garlic wafting
From room to empty room, the black cat
Rubbing herself against your bare leg
While you shuffle toward the distant light
And the tinkle of glasses in the kitchen.

One night, it was so hot in the bookstore where I was reading, I was soaked with sweat, my pants kept sliding down, so I had to hold them up with one hand while I held my book of poems in the other. Another time, I was reading in a nearly empty auditorium adjoining one in which the movie *King Kong* was being shown to a packed audience. At one point, during one of my quietest, most lyrical poems, I could hear the great ape growl as if he was on his way to strangle me. In a youth center in Queens, I was put on a program in the last minute between a magician and a mind reader and the audience was not told who I was and what I was supposed to be doing. I recall their bewildered expressions as I read my first poem. In Detroit, I had two babies howling while I read and then finally a lapdog somebody had sneaked in started to yelp. I was so drunk in Geneva, New York, I read over two hours, some of the poems twice, or so I was told afterward. After hearing my poem "Breasts," a dozen women walked out in Oberlin, each one slamming the door behind her. In a high school in Oregon I was introduced as the world-famous mystery writer Zimic. The shortest reading I ever gave lasted exactly twenty-eight minutes, whereas the crowd and the organizers expected a full hour. I had an excellent excuse. I squeezed the reading between the first and final quarters of a Celtics playoff game and had to rush back to my motel. In Ohrid, Macedonia, I read to an audience of thousands who did not understand English, but who nevertheless applauded after every poem. I ask you, how much more can one hope from life?

CHARLES SIMIC

Hal Sirowitz

Hal Sirowitz lives in Flushing, New York. Born in New York City, he grew up in East Meadow and Long Beach, Long Island. *Mother Said* (Crown), his first collection of poems, was published in 1996 and was an immediate success; a first printing of fifteen thousand copies—high for any poetry book—sold out quickly. The book became a best-seller in Norway. *My Therapist Said* followed two years later, also from Crown. Asked whether Franz Kafka had influenced him, Sirowitz replied, "He had trouble with his father. I relate to people who had trouble with their parents." He has been called "the unofficial poet laureate of Flushing." He read at KGB on May 11, 1998.

EQUALITY

We made love Then she cleaned
my ears with Q-tips. She showed
me the wax. She said she wanted
me to be able to hear what she
had to say. But I thought
that just like I had stuck
something into her she wanted
to stick something into me.

The worst poetry event I ever witnessed was one I had the misfortune to read at. It was at the Mudd Club, a punk club, in the early eighties. *High Times* magazine organized a benefit for Guru Ganja. Kathy Acker, the novelist, and I were the readers. While I was reading the Guru was smoking dope and dispensing advice. It was hard to find my rhythm while he talked.

Then I got hit by an empty beer bottle. I saw it coming from the corner of my eye, but I was in the middle of a stanza, so I wasn't able to duck. It bounced off my chest. I decided to cut my reading short. And when I complained to the organizer, he claimed it was a sign of affection. If I got hit by a bottle which still had beer in it, then I was being insulted. But since he finished the beer before he threw the bottle, he must have held me in high regard.

HAL SIROWITZ

Hal Sirowitz (left) tells David Lehman about his travels in Norway, where his books are bestsellers.

Charlie Smith

Charlie Smith was born in Moultrie, Georgia, in 1947. He grew up in the South, attended eastern schools, and settled in New York City. He has published four books of poems and six books of fiction, including *Before and After* (Norton) and *Cheap Ticket to Heaven* (Holt). His new book of poems is called *Heroin*. He read at KGB on April 13, 1998.

SANTA MONICA

Someone was writing this incredibly personal poem
and I was reading it over his shoulder
Santa Monica was in the poem
but you could hardly tell
and the devastating loss of integrity
his wife ranting
his cowardice—these were in the poem
and he was sweating as he wrote it
and looking around as if for spies
I am amazed he didn't see me
but sometimes they look right through you
he went on writing his act of contrition
and memory
expressing his extreme embarrassment and sorrow
at how he selfishly used loved ones, etc
lost the money and the house
sat in the car out in the driveway the last morning
and couldn't think where to go

until someone, a cop maybe, suggested
he go get something to eat, and then after that he drove
to Kansas. There was a weeping blue cypress in the poem
and at one point he was very accurate about how it feels
when on the street the beloved turns you away.
Sometimes, he wrote, *I stand unnoticed at a counter, waiting.*
At last the woman looks at me and asks what.
It was a struggle, for both of us, to get to the next part.

"What a night what a light what a moon/white with patches of blue snow & here I am/striding longlegged to the bar on East 4th Street/Never was a Martini more deserved."

Tomaz Salamun (left) and Gerald Stern embrace following their joint appearance at KGB in April 1999.

Mark Strand

Mark Strand was born in Canada of American parents in 1934. He is currently on the University of Chicago's Committee on Social Thought. He has held a MacArthur Fellowship and has served as the nation's poet laureate. He was the guest editor of *The Best American Poetry 1991*. He has published many books of poetry as well as short stories and translations from the Spanish and the Portuguese. His most recent collections of poems, all from Knopf, are *Blizzard of One* (1998), *Dark Harbor* (1993), and *The Continuous Life* (1990). He received the Pulitzer Prize in 1999. He read at KGB on March 12, 1998.

THE NIGHT, THE PORCH

To stare at nothing is to learn by heart
What all of us will be swept into, and baring oneself
To the wind is feeling the ungraspable somewhere close by.
Trees can sway or be still. Day or night can be what they wish.
What we desire, more than a season or weather, is the comfort
Of being strangers, at least to ourselves. This is the crux
Of the matter, which is why even now we seem to be waiting
For something whose appearance would be its vanishing—
The sound, say, of a few leaves falling, or just one leaf,
Or less. There is no end to what we can learn. The book out there
Tells us as much, and was never written with us in mind.

*Pulitzer Prize winners Mark Strand (left) and Richard Howard compare
experiences as poetry editors. At the time this photo was taken Strand
was editing poetry for* The New Republic *(Charles Wright has since
succeeded him). Howard continues to select the poems for*
The Paris Review.

Tony Towle

Tony Towle was born in New York in 1939. He became associated with the New York School of Poetry in the early 1960s and won the Frank O'Hara Award in 1970, in conjunction with which his book *North* was published. His most recent volume (of seven) is *Some Musical Episodes* (Hanging Loose Press, 1992). He has received fellowships from the National Endowment for the Arts and the Ingram Merrill Foundation and has read his work in some 250 venues since 1963. He lives in Tribeca (the "triangle below Canal Street") in New York City. He read at KGB on October 13, 1997.

POSTMODERN MATURITY

When Parliament passed the Onion Act of 1707
I thought it was the dumbest thing
I had ever heard of grown men doing,

until I gave in and sent off the five dollars
to join the American Association of Retired People —
or is it Persons? I don't want to be accused of Collectivism
at this point
on the stage of world history,

and Juvenal said that to appear on the stage at all
was a fate worse than death,
though he couldn't have known when he said it,

but of course he might have found out later,
and he nonetheless spoke from the clamorous stage of the Roman
    Empire,
which is now a faded and dusty backdrop for ours.

And other asterisks twinkle like stars overhead,
referring to so many of the dramatic remarks
uttered within civilized parentheses
that I will never get to them all . . .

but here the professor interposes:
Your utterance is neither credible nor concise.
I don't have to be credible or concise,
I'm a retired person. A *layabout,*
I think the English say,
adjusting their collective monocle;
and since I did not show up early enough
on the stage of world history
to actually now *retire,*
they send me *Postmodern Maturity* with my membership,
the AARP, that is, not the English,
so I can preview the relentless facts and articles,
and puzzling letters to the editor,
that are not yet quite relevant, but too soon will be.

Dear Postmodern Maturity:

I have just got back from the Depths (no modernist metaphor intended)
but yet I enjoyed your unspoken comparison of today's health-care costs

to those medieval crypts that increase in mysterious pungency as the cen-
turies pass.
But I would still like to see more discourse on the Great Platonic Brick.
You know the one I mean, the invisible support
for all the self-referential, daily-reality bricks
that hold up the scene even when you've missed your lines,
and at the same time is a disembodied token of the real reality
as it hurtles from offstage like a cartoon dénouement . . .

But here the layout person has intervened,
with an ad for pills
that are supposed to make 75-year-olds
feel like I do.
Save your money,
I want to tell them.
You don't know how well off you still are,
they answer.

And then the letter concludes:

. . . so when Parliament passed the Onion Act of 1707, I thought it was
the dumbest thing I had ever heard of grown men spending their time on.
But when it was followed by the Carrot Act, the Parsley Act, and then, in
1798,
the Great Potato Act, I realized that England was the center of an
immense
vegetarian conspiracy that continues to simmer in the soup the attendants
might bring me for lunch even today. But wait . . . there's the sound of the
tambourine cutting through the noodles again (no post-metaphoric
symbolism

intended) so I better sign off. By the way, how about an article on where
we came from, what we're doing here, and where we go afterwards. Please
do this soon, as I'm out of ideas and time is running out.

MRS. ESTHER BROWN, HAMILTON, OHIO

THANKS FOR THE LETTER, ESTHER, BUT WE FEEL THE HUMAN EPIC IS

    LIKE A GOOD

DETECTIVE STORY, SO WE WON'T BE THE ONES TO GIVE AWAY THE

    PLOT—

ESPECIALLY THE ENDING! BUT IF ANYONE CAN FIGURE IT OUT, WE'RE

    POST-IRONICALLY

SURE IT'S YOU.

THE EDITORS

And when I next glanced up from the magazine,
in the dressing room reserved for the Chronologically Advantaged,
life seemed to have lowered the lighting one more touch,
casting a less elusive shadow on the curtains
that part only for the Chronologically Overwhelmed.

To the Editors:

I spent a good deal of time, during my recent operation, trying to concep-
tualize
the above, "England" being the only reality-based allusion. But I think
the writer refers to the 1707 Act of Union between England and Scotland
rather than any mythical vegetarian conspiracy, although my doctor, as
he was rearranging my organs, suggested I join one.

ILLEGIBLE, NEW YORK CITY

NOT SO FAST, FRIEND. YOUR LETTER COULD NOT POSSIBLY HAVE BEEN

    PROCESSED QUICKLY

ENOUGH TO BE PUBLISHED IN THE SAME ISSUE AS WHAT YOU'RE

    REFERRING TO. IF YOU CAN'T

SUPPRESS THE URGE TO COMMUNICATE WITH US AGAIN, GET IT

    TOGETHER WITH THE SPACE/TIME

CONVENTIONS IN USE ON THIS PLANET SINCE AT LEAST THE

    COOLIDGE ADMINISTRATION.

THE EDS.

But here the professor intervenes once more.

"I told you," she admonishes, "that as soon

as you took your eye off life for just one more frivolity,

it would spin irrevocably away,

and leave you standing there

holding a ton of Platonic bricks;

"and that what you thought you would have at last figured out some day,

such as how to live with someone, or how to live, period,

will have by then slipped unattainably away

into the abyss."

    Postscript

To the Editors:

Like many of the readers that endure the fatigue of waiting to go

    backstage,

I swore I would not waste any more precious irritability

on cynical young editors who twist your words like tourniquets

to cut off your intent. But I have just read the foregoing—I guess it's what
you people call a text, isn't it—and my eyes are moist with tears.
Thanks for impinging momentarily on my consciousness.

Coda

And continuing on themselves, the asterisks have fallen to earth,
their referents disbanded. All these divagations have merely held off
for a few scant moments
my ongoing chronological calculations.
I wish you had seen fit to skip it all
and just publish the poem I submitted.
It was called "Edifying Tales of the Deep"
and I'll read it now.

It is thus a perfect time to watch the clouds go by,
and you tilt your chin to watch their diverse meanderings,
sensations dwindled to the sound of a lighting match,
but to illuminate . . . what, exactly? Memories, no doubt,
those most antic of God's phenomena,
frozen for much of the time,
but now blaring their microscopic trumpets
in a procession
you are no longer at the head of,
as if the poem had suddenly changed planes at Frankfurt
and let you off in a deserted field, near Syracuse, New York,
which dwindles to a tiny beanbag, with tinier writing on it; no,
nothing could be like that, really, and maybe
you'll edit that part out. While you do,

I continue my stalking of eternity,
treading mystic grains of time in the gravel of space. Wrinkles
have been found in the fabric of space, along with campfires
lit and abandoned by voluminous beings—
and these we call stars. They still throw light
on our past events, though not enough
to see what they were.

Tony Towle has been an important New York School presence since his
first book, North ("Your story is truly a story to treasure, distilled
intoxicant that it is,/saying that I am a synonym for the relaxed and
drifting universe"), won the Frank O'Hara Award in 1970.

John Tranter

John Tranter has published thirteen collections of verse, including *Selected Poems* in 1982, *The Floor of Heaven* (a book-length sequence of four verse narratives) in 1992, *Gasoline Kisses* (Equipage, Cambridge, U.K.) in 1997, and *Late Night Radio* (Polygon, Edinburgh) in 1998. *Different Hands* (Folio/Fremantle Arts Centre Press), a collection of seven experimental prose pieces, was published in 1998. His work appears in *The Norton Anthology of Modern Poetry*. He recently coedited the *Penguin Book of Modern Australian Poetry*, published in Britain and the United States as the *Bloodaxe Book of Modern Australian Poetry*. He is the editor of the free Internet magazine *Jacket*, at http://www.jacket.zip.com.au/welcome.html. He read at KGB on November 24, 1997.

MOONSHINE SONATA

I come to, knocking on the door of the cellar—
locked up for the summer—where you keep your "heart."
But isn't that the parcel you passed
to some likely guy, a neighborhood fellow,
one spring day full of showers and confetti,
in between mowing the lawn in a check shirt
and making sensible plans for your retirement?
Why don't you ask for it back, wrapped
in plastic—we could take it with us on our
vacation from the feelings we wade through
each evening, in our separate rooms.

                    Then I really
wake up, and there I am: painting
the skylight amber to filter the glare
that shines on the Southern Hemisphere,
and when the record stops, it's your turn:
Love & Marriage, say, or *Frenesi*,
but not the Moonshine Sonata
                    in his black jacket
gusting across Broadway in a flurry of snow.

David Trinidad

David Trinidad was born in Los Angeles in 1953. His books include *Answer Song* and *Hand over Heart: Poems, 1981–1988*. He currently teaches poetry at Rutgers University, where he directs the Writers at Rutgers series and is a member of the core faculty in the M.F.A. writing program at New School University. He writes: " 'Of Mere Plastic' is based on 'Of Mere Being' by Wallace Stevens. The first line ('The Barbie at the end of the mind') is from a book review by Wayne Koestenbaum. A play on Stevens's 'The palm at the end of the mind,' it inspired me to rewrite his poem, replacing his 'gold-feathered bird' with a blonde Barbie doll." He read at KGB on March 31, 1997.

OF MERE PLASTIC   for Wayne Koestenbaum

The Barbie at the end of the mind,
Beyond the last collectible, is dressed
In "Golden Glory" (1965–1966),

A gold floral lamé empire-styled
Evening dress with attached
Green chiffon scarf and

Matching coat with fur-trimmed
Neckline and sequin/bead
Detail at each side. Her accessories:

Short white gloves, clear shoes
With gold glitter, and a hard-to-find
Green silk clutch with gold filigree

Braid around the center of the bag.
It closes with a single golden button.
The boy holds her in his palm

And strokes her blonde hair.
She stares back without feeling,
Forever forbidden, an object

Of eternal mystery and insatiable
Desire. He knows then
That she is the reason

That we are happy or unhappy.
He pulls the string at the back
Of her neck; she says things like

"I have a date tonight!"
And "Let's have a fashion show
Together." Her wardrobe case

Overflows with the fanciest outfits:
"Sophisticated Lady," "Magnificence,"
        "Midnight Blue."
3 *hair colors. Bendable legs too!*

The doll is propelled through outer space,
A kind of miniature Barbarella.
She sports "Miss Astronaut" (1965),

A metallic silver fabric suit
(The brown plastic straps at the shoulders
And across the bodice feature

Golden buckles) and two-part
White plastic helmet. Her accessories:
Brown plastic mittens,

Zip boots, and sheer nylon
Mattel flag, which she triumphantly sticks
Into another conquered planet.

In the fall of 1981, Peter Schjeldahl was to give a reading from his new book *The Brute* at Beyond Baroque Literary/Arts Center in Venice, California. Dennis Cooper, who was directing events there, thought it would be a good idea if a few poets read before Schjeldahl, open reading style. I agreed to be one of them.

The night of the reading, I was in a morose mood. I'd just had a metal plate removed from my left leg, so I was on crutches. It didn't help that some of Schjeldahl's famous friends had shown up to hear him: John Travolta, Christopher Isherwood and Don Bachardy, the director James Bridges (*Urban Cowboy*), and Jack Larson (TV's Jimmy Olsen). Everyone else was excited by the celebrities; they only made me nervous and more morose. When Dennis introduced me, I hobbled toward the podium. Halfway there, someone in the cluster of celebrities laughed. I was devastated, but managed to get through a couple of poems. Every time I looked up at the audience, I saw John Travolta's head in the middle of the room.

Afterward, a friend said to me, "That was the worst reading you've ever given." I resented his honesty, but he was right.

DAVID TRINIDAD

The lovely Kim Savage began tending bar for us in September 1998.

Paul Violi

Paul Violi was born in New York City in 1944. His books of poems include *Splurge, Likewise, The Curious Builder,* and, most recently, *Fracas.* He has also produced three books in collaboration with the printmaker Dale Devereux Barker: *The Hazards of Imagery, The Anamorphosis,* and *Selected Accidents, Pointless Anecdotes.* He has been awarded two poetry fellowships from the National Endowment for the Arts, as well as grants from the New York Foundation for the Arts, the Fund for Poetry, and the Ingram Merrill Foundation. He teaches at Columbia and at New York University. He read at KGB on March 3, 1997.

THE HAZARDS OF IMAGERY

> *The frescoes in the castle are by Pisano, and they are so smooth and shining that even today you can see your own reflection in them.*
>
> —THE ANONIMO

AT THE CHAPEL CARDINAL FINALE

Here is a painting on wood
by an unknown hand,
of hearty fishermen in an open boat,
hauling a cow out of the Bay of Naples.
This painting smells:
an unfortunate odor no one
can eradicate or name.

Here, too, is a painting of the savior
from whose eyes many have attested
they have seen real tears fall.
And I for one believe it to be so.
For I have heard this said
of other paintings
and recalling how they are all
so unbelievably bad,
so poorly executed,
I have concluded that it is
the painters' utter ineptitude
that has made their very subject weep.
Such is the miraculous power of art.

IN THE GIFT SHOP AT THE LUNATIC ASYLUM

Always on sale, the figurines
of infants are made out of tar
and are produced by inmates,
former apprentices
of Imbrolgione mostly.
On visiting days family
and friends purchase them
as presents for the inmates.

IN THE BANCO GROSSO

Like many Romans
the ingenious Sprezzante,

the same who conceived
and designed the tollbooths
on the Via Dolorosa,
believed a tribute should display
the glory of the subject
without correcting his imperfections
or attempting to conceal them
from the eyes of the world.
Among his works here
is the snazzy life-like figure
of the surgeon Gianfrio,
who preferred to operate in the nude.
So tightly has the canvas
been stretched that the indignant,
the embittered, the vengeful,
are often re-injured
by the rebounding objects
they throw at it, and consequently
have to be taken back to the hospital.

AT THE TOMB OF THE
IMPROPERLY TRAINED BOMBARDIERS

This is the saddest work I have ever seen.
A tremendous concrete piano,
its maker unknown, yet—O soul of man!
Impenetrable silence!
The Great Echo!

The poems framed in the corridor
are by Maginot.
They are thick, the lines
impenetrable, true *vers Maginot*,
and visitors are advised
to simply go around them.

AT THE COTTAGE OF MESSER VIOLI

The mailbox, painted dark blue,
sits atop a tilted cedar post.
It has a little red flag on one side
and it is altogether remarkable.

The Toyota in the driveway
is very old and is said
to have come from Japan.

There is in the hallway
an immense dogfood bowl.
It is made of iridescent pink plastic.
It is, as I have said, immense
and it is hideous.

In the kitchenette is a statuette
of Ceres, Goddess of Wheaties.

The dishwasher is a Kenmore
and altogether worthy of praise.

In the foyer the over-sized painting
of a porkchop provides
visitors many opportunities
for conversation.

In the servants' quarters
there are many impressive works
that stress the imminence of death
and the probability of hell fire.

Placed on the broad maplewood table
beside bottles of cognac
there is a recording device
with a silver megaphone
into which natives are often
invited to shout
the oral histories of their people.

We whose hearts have been gripped
by life, scoff at the idea of art
as mere ornamentation: So they
seem to proclaim,
the three statues that adorn
the neighbor's lawn, plaster deer
with real bulletholes in them.

I gave a reading in June of 1981 at a library in Brewster. It lasted less than twenty minutes; getting there took forty. The librarian, when I reviewed arrangements with her over the phone, sounded unenthusiastic. So, a bit wary to begin with, I wasn't surprised when I walked in: no poster, no announcement, nobody. The woman on duty pleaded ignorance. She fished around her desk and found a check for me. I had the feeling that I was supposed to scoot, then heard someone mention "the poetry reading."

Five or six people were standing there. The one who asked about the reading hadn't come to hear it though, just accompany, or as he put it "deliver," the others. Introducing himself, he said he worked at an institution nearby, driving the "clients" to various community functions. His clients: five severely retarded adults. Two of them "subverbal," he explained, the others "semiverbal." I checked them out. The librarian, thinking she was doing me a favor, started to tell him the reading was off. For some reason, I cut her off.

Single file we went downstairs, carefully arranged chairs around a table, and sat. They checked me out. It was a very large room. The lighting was fine. They smiled at me, I smiled at them; I blinked, they didn't. They liked the way I opened my book. I opened another one. I led off with a short, slow poem. They look at, around, and over me. "Did any of that get through?" I asked. The driver had been staring at his shoes the whole time. Without looking up he said, "I doubt it."

I pulled out two more poems: an attempt at compressing—"squashing" might be a better word—a capitolo by Michelangelo and a rather literal translation of a sonnet by Cecco ("The Cynic of Sienna") Angiolieri. Both dramatic, vivid, forceful poems. If they didn't work . . .

They worked. Sort of. The scatological lines in the capitolo got a nod and a nervous laugh, a loud snort, and two full smiles. It's a very sad poem. I began the Angiolieri, known—as if nihilism needed an anthem—as "the Great Antisonnet." I aimed it at the client who I felt could talk in sentences and pick up the phrasing. I read the first stanza and stopped. I told him that when I began again I would read half a line and that he should finish it. I read half a line. I read it again and gestured to him. He caught on.

If I were fire . . . ?
I'd . . . put . . . you . . . out.
If I were wind . . . ?

I'd put on a coat?
If I were water . . . ?
I'd put on . . . another coat.
If I were God . . . ?
I'd put on another coat.
If I were *God*?
. . . I'd say . . . hello?

The others nodded, agreeing with his replies. He was taking a test and acing it. Then I read my translation.

"You liked that one?" They liked it. Sort of. "You like his better?" They liked his better.

The driver, who hadn't stopped looking at his shoes except to check his watch, then spoke: "Okay, now what do we say?" They said, almost in unison, "Thank you." "And now that we have to go, what do we do?" he prodded. They folded their green metal chairs and stacked them against the wall. "And now?" They fell in line and followed him up the stairs.

I wanted to hang around for a while. Maybe my audience had the same vague idea, or maybe it was clear to them. Something significant had happened. Nothing significant had happened. Sometimes a nice check tilts the balance. Sometimes not.

PAUL VIOLI

227

Paul Violi (left) broke up the audience with a poem spoofing the acknowl-edgments pages in poetry collections. In Violi's "Acknowledgments" we learn that Samuel Taylor Coleridge's "The Rime of the Ancient Mariner" appeared in Modern Bride *while the same poet's "Work Without Hope"* went to Popular Mechanics. *Here with Star Black. Photo: David Lehman.*

Karen Volkman

Karen Volkman was born in Miami in 1967. Her first book, *Crash's Law*, was published by Norton in 1996. Her poems have appeared in *The Paris Review*, *American Poetry Review*, *New American Writing*, and the 1996 and 1997 editions of *The Best American Poetry*. She lives in Brooklyn. She read at KGB on October 13, 1997.

CREATE DESIRE

Someone was searching for a Form of Fire.
Bird-eyed, the wind watched.
Four deer in a blowsy meadow.
As though it were simply random, a stately stare.

What's six and six and two and ten?
Time that my eye ached, my heart shook, why?
Mistaking lime for lemon.
Dressed in cobalt, charcoal, thistle—and control.

If they had more they would need less.
A proposal from the squinting logician.
Seems we are legal, seems we are ill.
Ponderous purpose, are you weather, are you wheel?

Gold with a heart of cinder.
Little blue chip dancing in the light of the loom.
Mistress, May-girl, whom will you kiss?
The death of water is the birth of air.

At KGB Karen Volkman (flanked here by poets Rick Meier and Barbara
Barg) read "Infernal," her dark vision of Miami: "The time her lover hit
her and she ran crying to the door / he said don't run out in the dark,
he said I'll drive you."

Bill ("April is the coolest month") Wadsworth. Designating April as
National Poetry Month was the brainchild of Wadsworth's Academy of
American Poets.

William Wadsworth

William Wadsworth was born in New York in 1950. He was educated at the University of Wisconsin and Columbia. His poems have appeared in *Grand Street, The New Republic, Shenandoah, The Yale Review,* and *The Paris Review.* He is executive director of the Academy of American Poets in New York City. He read at KGB on February 17, 1997.

THE NEED FOR ATTENTION

The angry boy takes out his realistic gun,

aims at the unfamiliar man and waits
to see what his mother will do. She shoots him a look.

The little girl at her birthday party shows off
her favorite doll and confides that she wants
to be bad so her daddy will spank her. You change the subject.

In those days Vietnam was a constant subject
of conversation. In those days, a cop with a gun
came to your house. You asked him what he wanted.
He told you not to move and your wife waited

for what she knew would come next. She was told to take off
her clothing so the authorities could look
at her breasts, her buttocks, her pubic hair. You look

away. You get angry. And the constant subject
gets personal. Ever since then your timing is off.

The popular hero arrives on the screen with a gun
poised like a salesman's handshake and waits
to find out what his friend the villain wants.
The villain knows precisely what he wants
which is why he's the villain. The hero begins to look
anxious. The ending is in the script. Why wait?

And so these words pursue their dangerous subject
like little heroes. The subject is a gun
intent upon the act of going off.
Now the hero flicks the safety off—
he's dying to ask us all what it is we want.

The villain cannot lose. He aims his gun
and gives the game his old habitual look.
He understands the innocence of his subject.
His timing is perfect. He's patient. He lies in wait.

While the mother dresses, the unfamiliar man waits.
He wonders what the babysitter wants
to talk about. What's her favorite subject?

The sitter turns the television off
and walks into the moonlight to look

for some affectionate sign that her life has begun.

She believes she knows what she wants while she waits.

The angry boy has drifted off with a gun.

The man says, look, in those days the war was an interesting subject.

Readings aren't normally life-or-death situations. Once, however, I was given the responsibility of introducing Salman Rushdie on the occasion of the American publication of *The Satanic Verses*. The reading was to be part of a literary series I ran at a theater in Manhattan and had been arranged well in advance of the controversy over the book. The event was to take place in February; over the course of the preceding fall my employers at the theater and I read accounts in the paper about riots, vandalism, and death threats surrounding the book's publication in England and India. But it wasn't until January, when we received a call from Rushdie's American publisher, that it dawned on us that some special preparations might be in order. The publisher, it turned out, had been receiving hundreds of bomb threats, and had come to the sensible conclusion that we should be alerted. My employers very bravely decided that we should not give in to censorship by intimidation, and that the show must go on.

The next few weeks were a short course in law-enforcement high-security tactics. After meeting with a special team of NYC detectives (called, I am not kidding, "the A-Team") and going over the finer points of entrances and exits ("We don't want to do the Jack Ruby Walk-Through," noted one of the A-Team), we were told about the three levels of security necessary in this situation: police outside the theater, airport weapons detectors and guards inside the entrance, and the A-Team themselves onstage with guns showing during the reading. This would be enough, they assured us, to discourage a single assassin, which—according to a helpful informant—was the only really likely scenario.

Then came the *fatwa*. A week before the reading, the Ayatollah

Khomeini issued his infamous death threat, and our informant called immediately, very agitated. No more single assassin: we were now to expect multiple assailants with automatic weapons and grenades. The A-Team, however, was only mildly fazed: "We'll alert the Delta Force," they said. This, we learned, was the name of the U.S. military's special forces team, trained to storm jets, kill terrorists, save hostages, et cetera. Thanks to the reassurances of the A-Team and the Delta Force, my employers announced that the reading was still on, no matter what. Resigned to my fate, I contacted my lawyer to update my will, rented a bulletproof vest—and vowed that if I survived this reading, I would stick from then on to introducing poets.

Fortunately, our plans proved unnecessary: two days before the reading, Rushdie canceled his trip to the States and went underground. Nevertheless, I did move immediately afterward to an organization where only poets are asked to read. I wish Mr. Rushdie well, but one of the reasons I love to attend readings at KGB is that it is unlikely the A-Team will ever be required there. In spite of the bar's sinister name, it has a dark crimson-walled smoky air of high security in the best sense: a virtual *womb* of poetry and good writing, a safe house of camaraderie and kinship between the writers and the audience. This is not a place to take for granted.

BILL WADSWORTH

Lewis Warsh

Lewis Warsh was born in New York City in 1944. His most recent books are a volume of stories, *Money Under the Table* (Trip Street Press, 1997); a book of poems, *Avenue of Escape* (Long News, 1995); a book-length poem, *Private Agenda*, with drawings by Pamela Lawton (Hornswoggle Press, 1996); and a memoir, *Bustin's Island '68* (Granary Books, 1996). He is currently editor and publisher of United Artists Books. He has taught at the Naropa Institute and Long Island University in Brooklyn. He has been a recipient of fellowships from the National Endowment for the Arts and the New York Foundation for the Arts. He read at KGB on March 9, 1998.

WHITE NIGHTS

The only thing we've lost
is seeing double
—Edwin Denby

We split a pill in two and walked in the Luxembourg Gardens until some gendarmes appeared on the side of a small hill and told us to leave. We held our breath in sleep among the pills and branches. There was cathair on the windowsill, like fleur-de-lys, and a light mist above the avenue surrounded by gates and fences. In a movie, not a musical or a comedy but something tragic and (somehow, at the same time) mundane, a man and his son were trying to escape over the Alps. They weren't fleeing the gendarmes, who seem harmless enough, babyfaced and cleanshaven, but someone more menacing and lacking what we think of as "conscience" (in the collective sense), so the moment you're caught by them you know you're going to die. I was standing on the sidewalk outside your apartment building waiting for you to throw down the key. The front door of the building was locked and there was no buzzer with your name on it. I was sitting at my desk, in the hour before dawn, copying words from a book. "A horse," I wrote, "represents God in the likeness of a horse." Then I looked up from my book and saw her face at the window. She had dark smudges on her cheekbones as if she had just climbed out of a mine and her hair was tied back in a way that made her look older than she was. In a movie, not a dream, a woman is waiting at home with her children for her husband to return from the mine. Instead, and this is the tragic part, one of his co-workers arrives to inform her that her husband died in an accident. In those days, mine accidents were a common occurrence, and the men who worked in the mine (there were no women mine-workers at that time) often died prematurely because their lungs were tainted with coaldust. It was no accident, or dream, but maybe it was a movie, where we met in a bar, fell in love, climbed the steps of a tenement, went to bed. We were just two people with our feet on the ground and hair on our heads, like everyone else. It was New Year's Eve but there were no more pills. It was late in the century, among the tenements and exit ramps, and we returned to the gardens where a posse of policemen were situated so that anyone entering or leaving had to present them with papers: passport, driver's license. We went uptown to get some pills from the doctor but he wasn't in and his assistant (a nurse with a cough) refused to write a new prescription. Some days copying words from books is safer and more reliable than talking to people and thinking about what they left out, all the secrets, a blur of sirens and wrong numbers. We searched the medicine cabinet for pills and when we couldn't find any we cursed in all the languages we knew until the people who lived downstairs complained about the noise and called the police. We drove through the night like migrant workers in a windowless van to a police station where a man in a uniform asked me to roll up my sleeves to check for needlemarks. The sky was the color of Chinese porcelain and we could see our reflections in every shopwindow. We split the last pill, licking the crumbs from our fingers. We checked our baggage into a locker at La Gare du Nord, converted our francs into marks, took a bus to the edge of the highway, and never looked back.

Susan Wheeler

Susan Wheeler was born in Pittsburgh, Pennsylvania, in 1955. Her books of poetry are *Smokes* (Four Way Books, 1998) and *Bag 'o' Diamonds* (University of Georgia Press, 1993), winner of the Poetry Society of America's Norma Farber First Book Award. Her work has appeared in five editions of *The Best American Poetry*. She teaches in the M.F.A. program in creative writing at New School University and in the department of English at New York University. She received a Guggenheim Fellowship in 1999. She read at KGB on September 29, 1997.

PRODUCE, PRODUCE

after Robert Frost

The thinnest meal on the slightest isle
Sustains but poorly. So: the file
Of men and women, mile and mile,

In consult with the wizened bat.
Plumes and boas're where it's at—
She won't remember saying that.

If hunger takes them to the coast,
They find a spectacle to toast.
Or several of their peers to roast.

Those that make it to the south
Are lucky to live thumb to mouth.
They might prefer the Catamount

Where greenish mountains freeze the nuts.
Though scavenging is an art that's bust
The ravenous can be beauty sluts.

Those lucky few who do adduce
The food that keeps them from the noose
Will crave on, too. Produce, produce.

My first year out of school, I found myself one evening each week at a mixed-security men's prison in Woodstock, Vermont, putting masters I'd dutifully typed into the slot of the rotating drum of a mimeograph machine, in a small room below an isolation cell. Hearing a presence nearby, the convict in solitary would set to wailing or yelling, and to clanging the metal of his cell. Then a guard would accompany me to a small room, called the *library* despite all evidence, where seven or eight men—most of these not much older than I—gathered to write poetry under the direction of a greenhorn.

I had been hired by the Vermont Council on the Arts as one of twelve artists, ranging from pianists to sculptors, to work with what the agency called "spec-pops," or "special populations," under the federal government's Comprehensive Employment and Training Act. I also went to nursing homes, to teenage drop-in centers, and to a minimum-security prison downstate. But at the Woodstock prison, the men struggling with their poems were incarcerated for more than possession charges; their poems revealed experiences I'd found best left on-screen. I was careful never to ask them what they were "in for," and my chief staff contact did not volunteer it.

This administrator was a woman, and she had agreed to my proposal for the workshop immediately: her son, she explained, was a poet who appeared regularly in *The New Yorker*—had I heard of him? Norman Dubie? So three months into the workshop, when I told her that, at a Christmas party in the midst of a blizzard, I had met a broadcaster for Vermont Public Radio who was interested in putting the prison writers on the air, she was game—perhaps gamer than I, since the broadcaster had also noted he had no mobile mikes: I would need to bring the writers directly to a local station. I knew the prison was short-staffed; if the prisoners were going to give a poetry reading on the radio, they would need to be released into my care for the hour's drive.

It was a clear, cold winter day. Three of the writers had been chosen as good risks by the administrator and, authorized, I drove the prison van. By now I thought I knew a great deal about each man—both what would make him rile and what would melt him, but I knew little, of course.

All three were terrified. The usually voluble one rode in unbreathing silence. The others found this unbearable, and one tried to joke, nervously. The third asked, "Will my mother hear me?"

I had rarely given readings myself, but I knew these feelings. Later, as the men sat in front of microphones, in the oppressive, listening silence, their voices cracked. The broadcaster was an encouraging presence, smiling at passages in their poems, but the writers were most aware of an audience they couldn't see—something vast and *out there*, and their own intimidating selves counted for nothing. This I knew, too, firsthand. And when the writers were finished recording, their triumph was unremarked but palpable. The ride back was quietly festive.

It was humbling. I was daunted by the paucity of my imagination, of the expectations for these men I had framed by my own fear. I think of them now whenever I have the need to imagine *my* audiences in their boxer shorts. *Lily-livered before the unknown,* I think, *like them.*

SUSAN WHEELER

Trevor Winkfield

Trevor Winkfield exhibits his paintings at the Tibor de Nagy Gallery in New York City. A monograph on his work, *Trevor Winkfield's Pageant*, was published by Hard Press in 1997. "Nature Study" is reprinted from his collected writings, *In the Scissor's Courtyard* (Bamberger Books, 1994). He read at KGB on October 6, 1997.

NATURE STUDY

As dusk fell, nurse went in to stoke up the fire and heat the children's formulae. Betty, seeing her chance, dismantled the lawnmower and put it back in the shed; then, flashlight in hand, she zig-zagged a route across the puckered asphalt, using upturned seedboxes as stepping stones.

As expected, she found her younger brother at the bottom of the garden engrossed in counting worm casts, casts which when you put your nose over them smelt of new magazines (or at least so he'd told her). The encroaching darkness hid her approach, and it was not until she accidentally bumped into the sundial that he became aware of her presence. Too late: before he had time to convulse his body into struggles, she had pinioned it between her thighs.

"Oh, Betty, Betty, don't tell, don't tell, please don't tell," he pleaded, a mixture of fear and shame creasing his soiled features.

She smiled on him contemptuously.

"All right, little one. I shan't say anything . . . not a thing. Just so long as we can play at bee magnets together."

"Oh, Betty," he said, or rather whimpered—as though resigning himself to some well-known but still disliked fate. From past experience he knew that it was useless to resist, and so accordingly he allowed his body to slacken in acceptance, enabling Betty to release her grip and drag his limp frame onto the crazy paving, where she propped it, back flat against the cold stone.

He was already shivering as she took a thermos out of her satchel and poured its syrupy contents over his knees, being careful not to spill any of it on her own clothes. Replacing the cork in the thermos, and the thermos in her satchel, she picked up her flashlight and ran to the edge of the shrubbery, crouching there in one of the scooped-out nettle patches.

From this safe vantage point she directed her torchlight through the gloom to pinpoint her brother's knees.

Within seconds these shiny domes were being divebombed by swarms of bees, until his entire body was covered in a moving mass of yellow and black blobs.

Betty settled back on her haunches.

"Fur coats," she muttered to herself contentedly, and switched off the beam.

After about half an hour she awoke to hear stifled sobs emanating from her brother's direction; much to her amazement she found him still conscious, though combed in various dots.

"Oh, sis, I wasn't a jelly spine, was I? I was really brave this time, wasn't I?"

"Yes, Jim, you were brave all right. You played the game just fine. In fact, Jim, you're a real tough nut, a real tough 'un." She knelt down beside him and pressed her lips against his fine-haired knees, chin like peach fuzz.

Sometimes now, on Winter evenings especially, they press slices of honeycomb against their shins, to remind themselves of what things might have been.

Charles Wright

Charles Wright was born in Pickwick Dam, Tennessee, in 1935. Educated at Davidson College, he served in the army for four years, then attended the Writers' Workshop at the University of Iowa. He lectured at the universities of Rome and Padua under the Fulbright program. He has received fellowships from the National Endowment for the Arts and the Guggenheim Foundation and won a PEN award for his translation of Eugenio Montale's *The Storm and Other Things*. He is a professor of English at the University of Virginia at Charlottesville, where he lives with his family. In 1996 the Lenore Marshall Poetry Prize was awarded to him for his book *Chickamauga* (1995). For *Black Zodiac* (Farrar, Straus and Giroux, 1997) he received the *Los Angeles Times* Book Prize, the National Book Critics Circle Award in poetry, and the Pulitzer Prize. *Appalachia* appeared in 1998. These three recent books will be published, with a seven-poem coda, in 2000 under the title *Negative Blue*. He read at KGB on March 12, 1998.

CICADA BLUE

I wonder what Spanish poets would say about this,
Bloodless, mid-August meridian,
Afternoon like a sucked-out, transparent insect shell,
Diffused, and tough to the touch.
Something about a labial, probably,

                        something about the blue.

St. John of the Cross, say, or St. Teresa of Avila.
Or even St. Thomas Aquinas,
Who said, according to some,
                    "All I have written seems like straw
Compared to what I have seen and what has been revealed to me."
Not Spanish, but close enough,
                    something about the blue.

Blue, I love you, blue, one of them said once in a different
        color,
The edged and endless
Expanse of nowhere and nothingness
                    hemmed as a handkerchief from here,
Cicada shell of hard light
Just under it, blue, I love you, blue . . .

We've tried to press God in our hearts the way we'd press a leaf
        in a book,
Afternoon memoried now,
                    sepia into brown,
Night coming on with its white snails and its ghost of the
        Spanish poet,
Poet of shadows and death.
Let's press him firm in our hearts, O blue, I love you, blue.

Charles Wright autographs a copy of Black Zodiac. *"The unexamined life's no different from/the examined life," he writes in the title poem. "You've got to write it all down." Long Island poetry impresario Faith Lieberman is in the right background.*

It Was the Worst of Times, It Was the Best of Times

Early December 1987. Wise County, southwest Virginia, deep in the hollows and broken hills of coal country. Clinch Valley College. I am to read my poems to the assembled multitudes this morning, after having done likewise the evening before in a packed room at the Wise County Regional Library. Showtime. My escort—an English professor about my age, who had invited me—and I arrive at the appointed room at the appointed hour. Empty. Not one body. Hmmm. A few minutes after the hour a young man appears. He's it. The audience. My escort wants to call the whole thing off and pay me on the spot. I demur, embarrassed almost beyond speech. I'll go on. Showtime. Suddenly the young man gets up and says he is going to get someone else. He leaves and returns in about two minutes with, as he tells us, his girlfriend. The three of us, the two students and I, sit at a long table, me on one side, the two students directly opposite, facing me. The escort takes a desk seat farther back in the room. I read from my poems for about forty-five minutes, the most relaxed and most pleasant reading experience I've ever had.

After the reading I began talking to the young man about contemporary poetry and poets. Or rather he to me. He knew everything and everyone. Amazing! How was this possible? And then I realized who he was, the poetry scapegoat for southwest Virginia. He had taken it all on his own head. He had come to the ceremony. He, of course, was the ceremony. Gratefully I sent him back into the wilderness.

CHARLES WRIGHT

C. K. Williams whispers the truth, the whole truth, and nothing but the truth in Marjorie Welish's ear after his KGB reading in May 1999.

Philip Levine during an intermission at KGB.

Acknowledgments

The editors wish to thank Denis Woychuk, principal owner of the KGB Bar, for his support. Without the industrious assistance of Mark Bibbins this book would have taken much longer to produce. Heartfelt thanks also go to our editor at Morrow, Taije Silverman, and to our literary agents, Glen Hartley and Lynn Chu. Mia Berkman made a valuable contribution.

Grateful acknowledgment is made of the literary periodicals and books in which some of these poems first appeared. Unless specifically noted otherwise, copyright to the poems is held by the individual poets.

Nin Andrews: "Poets on Poets" from *The Paris Review*. Reprinted by permission of the poet.

Sarah Arvio: "Mirrors" appears by permission of the poet. Copyright © 1999 by Sarah Arvio.

L. S. Asekoff: "Will" from *Dreams of a Work* by L. S. Asekoff. Copyright © 1994 by L. S. Asekoff. Reprinted by permission of the poet and Orchises Press.

John Ashbery: "New Constructions" from *The Yale Review* and *Wakefulness* by John Ashbery. Copyright © 1998 by John Ashbery. Reprinted by permission of the poet and of Farrar, Straus and Giroux.

Mary Jo Bang: "It Says, I Did So" from *Denver Quarterly*. Reprinted by permission of the poet.

Judith Baumel: "Snow-Day" from *Too Darn Hot: Writing About Sex Since Kinsey*. Judy Bloomfield, Mary McGrail and Lauren

Sanders, eds. Reprinted by permission of the poet and Global City Press/Persea Books. First published in *Global City Review*.

Erin Belieu: "Your Character Is Your Destiny" from *Meridian*. Reprinted by permission of the poet.

April Bernard: "See It Does Rise" from *Columbia: A Journal of Literature and Art*. Reprinted by permission of the poet.

Frank Bidart: "For the Twentieth Century" from *The Threepenny Review*. Reprinted by permission of the poet.

Walid Bitar: "Happy Hour" appears by permission of the poet. Copyright © 1999 by Walid Bitar.

Star Black: "Rilke's Letter from Rome" and "Personals" from *Sniper Logic*. "Hoopla" from *Yang*. "The Blank Abandon of Beds" from *Barrow Street*. These poems as well as "To a War Correspondent" and "Lust" appear here by permission of the poet.

Robert Bly: "The Day We Visited New Orleans" appeared in an earlier form in *Eating the Honey of Words: New and Selected Poems* by Robert Bly (Harper Flamingo, 1999). Reprinted by permission of the poet.

Tom Breidenbach: "Confessional" appears by permission of the poet. Copyright © 1999 by Tom Breidenbach.

Tom Carey: "Zohar" from *Hanging Loose*. Reprinted by permission of the poet.

Marc Cohen: "Evensong" from *Grand Street*. Reprinted by permission of the poet.

Billy Collins: "Tomes" from *Ploughshares*. Reprinted by permission of the poet.

Douglas Crase: "Astropastoral" appears by permission of the poet. Copyright © 1999 by Douglas Crase.

Carl Dennis: "St. Francis and the Nun" from *Poetry.* Copyright © 1998 by Carl Dennis. Reprinted by permission of the poet and the editor of *Poetry.*

Tom Disch: "The Agreement of Predicate Pronouns" from *A Child's Garden of Grammar.* Copyright © 1997 by Tom Disch. Reprinted by permission of the poet and the University Press of New England.

Denise Duhamel: "Sex with a Famous Poet" from *The Star-Spangled Banner.* Copyright © 1999. Reprinted by permission of the poet and Southern Illinois University Press.

Elaine Equi: "Autobiographical Poem" from *American Letters and Commentary.* Reprinted by permission of the poet.

Jonathan Galassi: "Argument" appears by permission of the poet. Copyright © 1999 by Jonathan Galassi.

Suzanne Gardinier: "Two Girls" from *The Best American Poetry 1996,* ed. Adrienne Rich. Reprinted by permission of the poet and the series editor of *The Best American Poetry.*

Dana Gioia: "Failure" from *The Hudson Review* (1996). Reprinted by permission of the poet.

Lucy Grealy: "Murder" appears by permission of the poet. Copyright © 1999 by Lucy Grealy.

Rachel Hadas: "In the Grove" appears by permission of the poet. Copyright © 1999 by Rachel Hadas.

Mary Stewart Hammond: "The GWB in the Rain" from *Stone and Steel: Paintings and Writings Celebrating the Bridges of New York City.* Paintings and editing by Bascove. Reprinted by permission of the poet and David R. Godine.

Bob Holman: "Performance Poem" from *El Templo* and *Stovepipe.* Reprinted by permission of the poet.

Virginia Hooper: "A Reading" appears by permission of the poet. Copyright © 1999 by Virginia Hooper. The poem first appeared in *Postmodern Culture* (Oxford University Press).

Richard Howard: "Mrs. Eden in Town for the Day" from *The New Yorker*. Reprinted by permission; copyright © 1997 by Richard Howard.

Marie Howe: "Sixth Grade" from *What the Living Do*. Copyright © 1997 by Marie Howe. Reprinted by permission of the poet and W. W. Norton and Co.

Lawrence Joseph: "When One Is Feeling One's Way" appears by permission of the poet. Copyright © 1999 by Lawrence Joseph.

Vickie Karp: "Harm" from *A Taxi to the Flame*. Copyright © 1999 by Vickie Karp. Reprinted by permission of the poet and the University of South Carolina Press. Originally in *The New Yorker*.

Karl Kirchwey: "Oracular Degeneration" appears by permission of the poet. Copyright © 1999 by Karl Kirchwey.

Wayne Koestenbaum: "Gaudy Slave Trader" from *The Milk of Inquiry*. Copyright © 1999 by Wayne Koestenbaum. Reprinted by permission of the poet and Persea Books. First published in *The Antioch Review*.

Yusef Komunyakaa: "Chastity Belt" from *The Kenyon Review*. Reprinted by permission of the poet.

Wendy Wilder Larsen: "Bluebird in Cutleaf Beech" appears by permission of the poet. Copyright © 1999 by Wendy Wilder Larsen.

Ann Lauterbach: "The Novelist Speaks" from *American Letters and Commentary* (1998). Reprinted by permission of the poet.

David Lehman: "The Prophet's Lantern" from *Boulevard* (1998). Reprinted by permission of the poet.

Rika Lesser: "Translation" from *Growing Back: Poems 1972–1992*. Copyright © 1997 by Rika Lesser. Reprinted by permission of the poet and University of South Carolina Press. First published in *Poetry*.

Thomas Lux: "Plague Victims Catapulted over Walls into Besieged City" appears by permission of the poet. Copyright © 1999 by Thomas Lux.

Elizabeth Macklin: "The House Style" from *Open City*. Reprinted by permission of the poet. The note on Linda Hunt's reading of Emily Dickinson is from "It's a Woman's Prerogative to Change Her Mind," in *By Herself*, ed. Molly McQuade. Reprinted by permission of Graywolf Press.

Pierre Martory: "Blues" from *The Landscape Is Behind the Door*. Copyright © 1994 by Pierre Martory and John Ashbery. Reprinted by permission of John Ashbery, translator and literary executor for Pierre Martory, and the Sheep Meadow Press.

Donna Masini: "Two Men, Two Grapefruits" appears by permission of the poet. Copyright © 1999 by Donna Masini.

J. D. McClatchy: "Bishop Reading" was written on the occasion of this anthology and appears by permission of the poet. Copyright © 1999 by J. D. McClatchy.

Honor Moore: "A Window at Key West" from *The Paris Review*. Reprinted by permission of the poet.

Paul Muldoon: "Hard Drive" from *The Sunday Times* (London). Reprinted by permission of the poet.

Eileen Myles: "Milk" from *Jacket*. Reprinted by permission of the poet.

Charles North: "Philosophical Songs" from *Columbia: A Journal of Literature and Art* (New York) and *Columbia Poetry Review* (Chicago). Reprinted by permission of the poet.

Vijay Seshadri: "The Scholar" from *The New Yorker*. Reprinted by permission; copyright © 1997 by Vijay Seshadri.

David Shapiro: "Old Poems" from *Exact Change Yearbook #1*, eds. Peter Gizzi and Michael Palmer. Reprinted by permission of the poet.

Harvey Shapiro: "6/20/97" from *Boulevard*. Reprinted by permission of the poet.

Charles Simic: "The Lives of Alchemists" from *The London Review of Books*. Reprinted by permission of the poet.

Hal Sirowitz: "Equality" appears by permission of the poet. Copyright © 1999 by Hal Sirowitz.

Charlie Smith: "Santa Monica" is used by permission of the poet.

Mark Strand: "The Night, The Porch" from *Blizzard of One*. Copyright © 1998 by Mark Strand. Reprinted by permission of the poet and Alfred A. Knopf.

Tony Towle: "Postmodern Maturity" from *Hanging Loose* and *Blade* (Isle of Man). Reprinted by permission of the poet.

John Tranter: "Moonshine Sonata" appears by permission of the poet. Copyright © 1999 by John Tranter.

David Trinidad: "Of Mere Plastic" from *Pearl*. Reprinted by permission of the poet.

Paul Violi: "The Hazards of Imagery" from *Fracas*. Copyright © 1999 by Paul Violi. Reprinted by permission of the poet and Hanging Loose Press.

Karen Volkman: "Create Desire" from *Verse*. Reprinted by permission of the poet.

William Wadsworth: "The Need for Attention" from *Shenandoah*. Reprinted by permission of the poet.